bonnie & mahesh
CHAVDA

# The
# HIDDEN POWER
## of a

# WOMAN

**Destiny Image® Publishers, Inc.**
**P.O. Box 310**
**Shippensburg, PA 17257-0310**

ISBN 10: 0-7684-2352-X
ISBN 13: 978-0-7684-2352-5

*"Speaking to the Purposes of God for this Generation
and for the Generations to Come."*

This book and all other Destiny Image, Revival Press, MercyPlace, Fresh Bread, Destiny Image Fiction, and Treasure House books are available at Christian bookstores and distributors worldwide.

For a U.S. bookstore nearest you, call
**1-800-722-6774.**

For more information on foreign distributors, call
**717-532-3040.**

Or reach us on the Internet:
**www.destinyimage.com**

1 2 3 4 5 6 7 8 9 10 11 / 09 08 07 06

*YHWH, God, built the rib that He had taken*
*from the human into a woman*
*and brought her to the human.*
*The human said:*
*This time, she is it!*
*She shall be called woman*
*And the woman saw that the tree was good for eating*
*And that it was a delight to the eyes*
*And the tree was desirable to contemplate.*
*She took from its fruit and ate*
*And gave also to her husband beside her,*
*And he ate.*
*And the eyes of the two of them were opened*
*And they knew…*

# Dedication

*This book is dedicated to Laxmiben and Anna Gwynn, our mothers who nurtured us with their law before we knew the law of God.*

# Contents

# Part One

## The Hidden Power of Eve

# Chapter One

# The Daughter of a Lion

In June 2005 three lions rescued a twelve-year-old girl in Ethiopia from seven men who had kidnapped her a week earlier. They had subjected her to repeated beatings in an effort to force her to marry one of the men. Abducting young girls for marriage is a long-standing custom in Ethiopia, particularly in the rural areas where most of the nation's people live.

Local custom was stood on its head this day as the seven kidnappers were suddenly confronted by the three lions that appeared out of the forest. The lions chased away the girl's captors and then stayed with her for half a day until rescuers arrived. According to one rescuer, a police sergeant, "They stood guard until we found her and then they just left her like a gift and went back into the forest. If the lions had not come to her rescue, then it could have been much worse. Often these young girls are raped and severely beaten to force them to accept the marriage." A local government official agreed, saying, "Everyone thinks this is some kind of miracle, because normally the lions would attack people."[1]

Something is happening for women. Even nature is speaking to us through the miraculous deliverance of this young woman by the three lions. Could it be a sign that the Lion of the tribe of Judah is arising to defend His handmaidens in this hour? We believe He is.

The whole incident sounds strangely and wonderfully like a foretaste of the "peaceable kingdom" described by the prophet Isaiah:

> The wolf also shall dwell with the lamb, the leopard shall lie down with the young goat, the calf and the young lion and the fatling together; and a little child shall lead them. The cow and the bear shall graze; their young ones shall lie down together; and the lion shall eat straw like the ox. The nursing child shall play by the cobra's hole, and the weaned child shall put his hand in the viper's den. They shall not hurt nor destroy in all My holy mountain, for the earth shall be full of the knowledge of the Lord as the waters cover the sea.[2]

The day is coming when the whole of creation, fractured, marred and divided as it is by the sin of mankind, will be whole again, restored to peace and harmony by the redemptive work of Jesus Christ when He shed His blood and gave His life on the cross. All creation waits with bated breath for that day:

> For the earnest expectation of the creation eagerly waits for the revealing of the sons of God. For the creation was subjected to futility, not willingly, but because of Him who subjected it in hope; because the creation itself also will be delivered from the bondage of corruption into the glorious liberty of the children of God. For we know that the whole creation groans and labors with birth pangs together until now.[3]

## God's Sons and Daughters

What will usher in the restoration of creation? The "revealing of the sons of God." And who are the "sons of God"? All who possess and are led by the Spirit of God. This means men *and* women, male *and* female, because the word "sons" here is gender-inclusive. Paul makes this whole relationship between the revealing of God's "sons" and the restoration of creation quite clear in the contextual passages surrounding the verses above:

> *For as many as are led by the Spirit of God, these are sons of God. For you did not receive the spirit of bondage again to fear, but you received the Spirit of adoption by whom we cry out, "Abba, Father." The Spirit Himself bears witness with our spirit that we are children of God, and if children, then heirs—heirs of God and joint heirs with Christ, if indeed we suffer with Him, that we may also be glorified together.*
>
> *For I consider that the sufferings of this present time are not worthy to be compared with the glory which shall be revealed in us.*[4]

All who possess the Spirit of God, the "Spirit of adoption," have been adopted as children of God, heirs to His Kingdom and joint heirs with Christ. Again, this includes male *and* female; *all* of God's children—His sons *and* His daughters. We too are "eagerly waiting for the adoption, the redemption of our body" on that great day when all things will be restored to God's original design and purpose.

## Make Their Presence Known

All of this, our adoption, redemption and the restoration of creation, is made possible by the atoning death of Jesus Christ, the *"Lion of the tribe of Judah."*[5] Paul calls Him the *"firstborn among many brethren,"*[6] the "firstborn of creation"[7] and the *"firstborn"* from the dead. As the "firstborn," Christ is our Elder Brother, and if He is a Lion then we, in a sense, are lions, too. Lions make their presence known.

Mahesh grew up in Africa and remembers well the sound of roaring lions in the jungles surrounding the town where he lived. It was not an uncommon event for lions to cross the bridge into town and wander down the streets, their mighty roars striking fear into the hearts of all who heard them.

The day is coming when God's lions and lionesses are going to roar and make their presence known. It has, in fact, already happened. On the day of Pentecost, 50 days after Jesus' resurrection, the Holy Spirit descended upon 120 believers gathered in that upper room in Jerusalem, thus fulfilling Joel's prophecy of hundreds of years earlier:

> And it shall come to pass afterward that I will pour out My Spirit on all flesh; your sons and your daughters shall prophesy, your old men shall dream dreams, your young men shall see visions. And also on My menservants and on My maidservants I will pour out My Spirit in those days.[8]

Filled with the Spirit, those 120 "lions of God" poured into the streets of Jerusalem and "roared" the good news of the gospel of Christ in languages they had never learned, striking holy fear into everyone who heard them. By the end of the day, 3,000 people had been brought into the Kingdom of God.

It happened again on January 1, 1901, the very first day of the 20th century. Agnes Ozman, a Bible student of Holiness evangelist and faith healer, Charles F. Parham, became the first person (and *woman*!) in modern times to receive the baptism of the Holy Spirit with the evidence of speaking in tongues, thus inaugurating the modern Pentecostal movement. Reports indicate that Miss Ozman, who had never left the Midwestern region where she grew up, spoke in Chinese (and *nothing* but Chinese) for three days. During this time she also wrote only in Chinese characters. Soon after, the rest of Parham's students, as well as Parham himself, also received the baptism of the Holy Spirit and spoke in tongues.

*When the time came for God's lions to roar again, He chose one of His **daughters** to be the catalyst!*

There is an old Swahili proverb—"Binti wa simba na simba"—that means, "The daughter of a lion is also a lion." Lions make their presence known. They have a voice that cannot be silenced. Agnes Ozman's baptism in the Spirit with speaking in tongues was more than just the inaugural act of the modern Pentecostal movement. It was also a prophetic sign that the voice of women—God's lionesses—which had been repressed, restricted and silenced in the church for so long, was being restored.

## It's Time for God's Lionesses to Roar

The Spirit of the Lion is coming upon God's daughters and handmaidens. God's end-time lionesses are going to roar once again. Women through the ages have suffered and continue to suffer much oppression and suppression. This is due partly to culture, partly to prejudice and is partly self-inflicted as the result of a poor self-image. Our goal in this book is to help release the daughters of the Lion of the Tribe of Judah into their legitimate place and ministry of doing the works of Jesus as described in the Gospel of Luke:

> *The Spirit of the Lord is upon Me, because He has anointed Me to preach the gospel to the poor; He has sent Me to heal the brokenhearted, to proclaim liberty to the captives and recovery of sight to the blind, to set at liberty those who are oppressed; to proclaim the acceptable year of the Lord.*[9]

Jesus was reading from Isaiah chapter 61, which goes on to say:

> *To proclaim the acceptable year of the Lord, and the day of vengeance of our God; to comfort all who mourn, to console those who mourn in Zion, to give them beauty for ashes, the*

19

*oil of joy for mourning, the garment of praise for the spirit of heaviness; that they may be called trees of righteousness, the planting of the Lord, that He may be glorified." And they shall rebuild the old ruins, they shall raise up the former desolations, and they shall repair the ruined cities, the desolations of many generations... Instead of your shame you shall have double honor, and instead of confusion they shall rejoice in their portion. Therefore in their land they shall possess double; everlasting joy shall be theirs...I will greatly rejoice in the Lord, my soul shall be joyful in my God; for He has clothed me with the garments of salvation, He has covered me with the robe of righteousness, as a bridegroom decks himself with ornaments, and as a bride adorns herself with her jewels.*[10]

This mission and this *anointing* are for *all* of God's children; His sons *and* His daughters; His lions *and* His lionesses alike. In this book we want to address primarily the lionesses of God. God's intended destiny for every one of you, women made in His resemblance, replica, and likeness, is glorious, victorious and righteous.

The *shekinah*, the bright cloud outshining from God, shows forth His image. That glory is *weighty*; it has substance, authority, power and is the essence of the fruit of His righteousness. So majestic is that glory that a man or woman could die just from beholding it. We were created to reflect this same image of God. The very purpose of the anointing and the work of the Holy Spirit is to make us like Jesus, "the brightness of His glory and the express image of His person,"[11] doing Jesus' work and reflecting His image here on earth. Yet many women see themselves like the woman with the spirit of infirmity in Luke chapter 13: bent over and having exhausted her resources in an unsuccessful attempt to straighten up. For centuries women have sought to come out from under the yokes and limitations that have been forced upon them.

But now is the time of the new thing God has ordained to show forth His glory in the earth. The Third Person of the Godhead is at work to heal, build and show forth His glory in the personhood and self-image of every woman! You have been set apart as vessels of that glory. This is your glorious hour. This is the day of loosing you from every limitation you have put on yourself; the set time of being liberated from every restriction others have put on you because you are a woman. The time for spending all you have on self-help-extreme-makeover-feminist-political-action-counsel is over!

Your answer lies in the one and only source able to break this yoke: the *anointing* of God! The outpoured Holy Spirit through the good news of the gospel is for *you* in all its fullness! God created you in His image and ordained you to show forth that image. Woman, arise! Show yourself! Make your presence known! Throw off your former begging garments and be made whole! Your hour has come! Your day is here! It is time to enter into your inheritance as true daughters of the King! It is time for you to touch His presence and receive your restoration!

## All Men and Women are Created Equal

Unfortunately, too many of the King's daughters today have lost sight of their inheritance. Some are barely even aware of it while others have been shot down repeatedly in trying to claim it until they have all but given up. Prejudice, ignorance, misinterpretation, erroneous teachings, tradition and other factors prevent many of God's royal daughters from taking their rightful place in His plan and His Kingdom. In most cultures women are seen in a distinctly second-class and subservient role as compared to men. Even in the so-called "enlightened" nations of the West, women still struggle against inequality and many vestiges of patriarchal tradition that would hold them back from full participation in society as men's equals.

It hasn't always been this way. God never intended for His daughters to occupy a secondary place. And today He is hard at work bringing restoration so that His lionesses can return to their rightful place.

Genesis chapter 1 makes it perfectly clear that in the beginning woman was equal to man in every way—in intelligence, in authority, and in dominion:

> *So God created man in His own image; in the image of God He created him; male and female He created them. Then God blessed them, and God said to them, "Be fruitful and multiply; fill the earth and subdue it; have dominion over the fish of the sea, over the birds of the air, and over every living thing that moves on the earth."*[12]

God created man, male and female, in His image and gave *them* dominion over the created order. The essential equality of man and woman is brought out even further in the second chapter:

> *And the Lord God said, "It is not good that man should be alone; I will make him a helper comparable to him."...And the Lord God caused a deep sleep to fall on Adam, and he slept; and He took one of his ribs, and closed up the flesh in its place. Then the rib which the Lord God had taken from man He made into a woman, and He brought her to the man. And Adam said: "This is now bone of my bones and flesh of my flesh; she shall be called woman, because she was taken out of Man."*[13]

God *made* woman to be a *helper* for man. The Hebrew word for "made" literally means "built" while the word "helper" means a counterpart called "over against" or alongside, contributing vital aid or assistance. This is the same meaning as the Greek word *parakletos*, which is used in the New Testament as a reference to the Holy Spirit and is variously translated as Comforter,

Counselor and Helper.[14] Literally, *parakletos* means "called to one's side." Jesus sent Him to take the empty place beside us. In the same way, the role of the woman in relation to the man is similar to the role and ministry of the Holy Spirit in the lives of believers. The Holy Spirit exemplifies particular qualities and functions in power which are quintessentially innate to women. We could say that there are feminine characteristics found in the Godhead. In the history of patriarchy the idea of anything female being directly akin to God makes many uncomfortable. That is exactly what satan hopes.

The exclusion of the woman from spirituality in power, particularly in Judeo-Christian culture, has given way to two opposing extremes. On the one hand, women have been largely excluded from roles of spiritual power in many religions, most specifically Judaism, Christianity, and Islam. On the other, woman has been deified in the goddess religions and exalted to perversion by the feminist movement. Both are the antithesis of woman as created by God in God's image. In Judaism, unlike Christianity, God has never been viewed as exclusively male or masculine. Judaism has always maintained that God has both masculine and feminine qualities; in fact His redemptive names indicate just that. El-Shaddai, for instance, is the breasted One, illustrating God's nature as the nourisher of life in the way a mother nurses her child. The Old Testament often ascribes feminine characteristics to God as the protector-nurturer who said, *"Can a woman forget her nursing child? Yea though she may yet I have not forgotten you O Israel."*[15]

The Holy Spirit and women have a similar history. It is a story of unrecognized value and unspent power. Where the Spirit of the Lord is there is liberty. And where He is not welcome often it is the women who suffer the most. The history of the outpouring of God's Spirit in the old and new covenants has always figured women as prominent figures. The great debut was on the day of Pentecost and the fulfillment of Joel's prophecy. In those early days the lives of women changed dramatically. Theology of the Holy Spirit is somewhat non-existent in much of Judaism. The *shekinah* is the nearest symbolism. Present in Eden, at Sinai, in the Tabernacle, and the Temple over the ark, the *shekinah* is seen as God's "wife," as the outshining of His glory. This concept is consistent with Paul's saying in the New Testament about a woman being the "glory" of the man. The *shekinah* and the Temple are connected to one another. In the present without a Jewish Temple, the *shekinah* is said to be "in exile." A man who keeps Torah is expected to "cleave" to the *shekinah* when he travels from his home and wife until the couple is together again. When God told Adam to "cleave" to Eve, He provided the atmosphere whereby God would come and dwell and commune with the human. Woman was created as a carrier of this glory, and she is an integral part of the restoration of the glory on the earth as prophesied by Habbakuk.[16] In the first "exile" of the *shekinah*, when the ark of the covenant is captured by the Philistines, we see a picture of God's redemptive work in using the female to restore His glory to His people. In an action that showed forth the supernatural power of God, the Philistines place the ark of the covenant on a new cart, *"take two milk cows which have never been yoked, and hitch the cows to the cart; and take their calves home, away from them... Then the cows headed straight for the road of Beth Shemesh, and went along the highway, lowing as they went, and did not turn aside to the right hand or the left."*[17] God used these female cows and their sensitivity to His presence to restore the *shekinah* to Israel. The work of pulling the cart was foreign to them, yet these mother cows went against the desires of their flesh and natural inclination, submitting to the rulership of God's will and purpose. It is a picture of the redeemed bride as she comes into her identity as a carrier of the *shekinah* as an equal partner in the end-time purposes of God to show forth His glory on the earth.

God "custom-built" woman to be an exact, equal, and perfect counterpart to the man. He fashioned Eve from one of Adam's ribs, from his side, which is appropriate for one made to stand by his side as an equal partner. According to Jewish tradition, "The woman came out of a man's rib. Not from his feet to be walked on. Not from his head to be superior, but from the side to be equal. Under the arm to be protected, and next to the heart to be loved."

## But Men and Women are Also Different

The Jewish Oral Tradition adds some additional and intriguing insight into the original relationship between man and woman. Genesis chapter 1 refers to man in the *plural*, even before the record of Eve: "...*male and female He created* **them**." According to Jewish tradition, the plural is used because the first human was really an androgynous being, both male and female in one body, unified, whole, and self-sufficient. God later divided this being into two—male and female—not only so Adam wouldn't be alone, but also so that he wouldn't develop an attitude of self-sufficiency that might lead him to think that he did not need God. Jewish tradition has no concept of independence from God. God fashioned the human being into two separate people so that they would depend on each other, yearn for each other and give mutually to each other. Full realization of human spirituality is impossible alone.

Whether Jewish tradition concerning Adam's original physical form is correct or not, Eve, the woman, was intended from the beginning. They, both man *and* woman, were fashioned in the image of God. Creating two identical beings would not be sufficient because maximized giving requires that the recipient and the giver be different. Identical beings would have identical needs and wants. Distinct and separate beings would have different needs and wants, and each would learn to be sensitive to those of the other. Our differences teach us to appreciate, love, give and care for each other with respect and dignity. We see this "image of God" in the relationship of the Godhead, Father to Son, Son to Spirit, Spirit to Father.

Despite some modern notions to the contrary, true gender differences do exist. Men and women are different, not just in how they look but also in how they think. The oral tradition says the fact that Eve was made from an internal member of the man—his rib—signifies that feminine strength and nature focus more on the internal while the masculine focuses more on the external. In other words, women in general place much greater weight than men on relationships. It is interesting to note that the Hebrew word used for "rib" in the creation account is the same word used for the staves which upheld the curtained walls of the tabernacle, housing the golden furnishings and containing the *shekinah*. In like manner, women and their relational nature are essential to the very structure and framework of the Body of Christ.

Genesis describes the creation of Eve as "God-built." The Hebrew root, *binah*, means "insight" or "understanding." This suggests that God created women with an extra dose of wisdom and understanding. *Binah* means more than just "women's intuition." It refers to the ability to enter something and understand it from the inside, or by "inner reasoning." Binah is the wisdom of women, an internal partnership between the intuition built into her in the image of God and her intellect working together to sum up a situation. Women have an innate "nose" for discerning whether a situation, a person, or a plan is everything it should be. This gift was what Eve ignored in the Fall; listening instead to the serpent and following her own desires she was deceived. Yet God had equipped her with everything she needed not to be taken in. Men generally have *da'at*, an external type of understanding that is more related to facts and figures. In simple terms think right brain/left brain. When both are working together with the Holy Spirit, two can chase ten thousand. This is one of the principles of restoring the woman's voice. Her voice is her influence and power.

The critical nature of *binah* in the purpose of God is exemplified on several occasions as God used the voice of women to shape the formation and destiny of His people Israel. Both Sarah and Rebekah used their ability to discern the inner workings of the heart to direct the spiritual inheritance and blessing to the son of God's choosing, the son that carried the seed of promise in his character. When Abraham balked at sending away Ishmael, God interceded on Sarah's behalf, saying, "Listen to her voice." Even the great prophet Samuel was unable to discern the Anointed One of Israel and was corrected for looking only at the external attributes of Jesse's sons. God told him, "...*man looks at the outward appearance, but the Lord looks at the heart.*"[18]

This should make it clear that men and women are completely equal but also different—and that difference is good. God had Eve in mind from the start: separate, equal, different and compatible. She was fully woman, formed of the same primal substance and built into the perfect helper fit for man. God created two genders so that each could complement and fulfill the other. Men and women need to learn to appreciate and use their unique, special strengths. The important thing in all of this for women is the realization that they can be free to be themselves and can grow morally and spiritually while maximizing their unique strengths with self-esteem and joy—without apology.[18]

## It All Began with Eve

Woman as created enjoyed a high and exalted place of honor, blessing and authority alongside the man. But what happened? What changed so that much of the history of women is characterized by oppression, repression, suppression, and silencing? How did things get this way? It all started when the "mother of all the living" listened to the tempter.

When Eve listened to the voice of the serpent in the Garden of Eden, his words led her to question God. Her resulting rejection of God's commands caused her to lose her queenly authority and dominion. Likewise, Adam entered condemnation when he listened to the voice of his wife and ate that which God had prohibited.

In the beginning God created Adam and Eve—male and female—as the fullest expression of His creativity and pleasure. They were unique from all other creation because they were made in the likeness and image of God Himself and could therefore enter into a deep and personal love relationship with their Creator. Inbreathed with the "rushing-Spirit" of God, they were given dominion over everything else that God had made.[20]

They were *not*, however, given dominion *over each other*. Adam and Eve were equal partners in dominion as vice-regents of God over the created order. God gave them only one prohibitive command as a test of their love and their willingness to obey: "*Of every tree of the garden you may freely eat; but of the tree of the knowledge of good and evil you shall not eat, for in the day that you eat of it you shall surely die.*"[21]

One day the tempter engaged Eve in conversation in which he called God's integrity into question:

> *Now the serpent was more cunning than any beast of the field which the Lord God had made. And he said to the woman, "Has God indeed said, 'You shall not eat of every tree of the garden'?" And the woman said to the serpent, "We may eat the fruit of the trees of the garden; but of the fruit of the tree which is in the midst of the garden, God has said, 'You shall not eat it, nor shall you touch it, lest you die.'"*
>
> *Then the serpent said to the woman, "You will not surely die. For God knows that in the day you eat of it your eyes will be opened, and you will be like God, knowing good and evil." So when the woman saw that the tree was good for food, that*

*it was pleasant to the eyes, and a tree desirable to make one wise, she took of its fruit and ate. She also gave to her husband with her, and he ate. Then the eyes of both of them were opened...* [21]

The serpent held out to Eve a very tempting lure: the chance to become "like God." Eve thought for a moment and then said, "Okay, I'll bite." And she did—literally! Then she turned to Adam, held out the fruit and said, "Come on, honey, try this one!" He did, and it was all over. Eve listened to the tempter and lost her authority and dominion. Adam listened to his wife and fell right along with her.

God's judgment was swift. He cursed the serpent for his deception, and He cursed the ground so that only through hard toil and labor would man be able to make the soil produce the food he would need to live. This was in direct contrast to the abundant fertility and fruitfulness of Eden.

God made two announcements regarding the woman. He said, "I will greatly multiply your sorrow and your conception; in pain you shall bring forth children." Prior to their separation from God, it appears the advent of every human child was to be an extraordinary celebration of significance and joy. Each new human was to be built within the body of the woman, fashioned by a design only she carried within. The emphasis of the dread pronouncement "in pain shall you bring forth children" has all but trivialized the fact that woman retained the power of life originally given her. That power was compromised, she sold her birthright so to speak, but even then, God never removed her power of life. She still carried the Seed. God continued, *"Your desire shall be for your husband, and he shall rule over you."* [23] Woman wants in—into the heart, into the conversation, into the decision-making. This is from God, for as man's helper she was designed to be *in*-volved! The break that took place in the community of God and man through man's disobedience also broke the communion between the man and the woman. Their oneness was now restricted to the body; the spirit bond now absent, they would strive with one another to communicate—to have dominion. *Male domination of women in general and husband's domination of their wives in particular are consequences of the Fall,* **not** *part of God's original purpose and design!* Desire was a God-given element by which we were to rule and have dominion. In intimate communion with Him, our desires would always be submitted to His. However, when the serpent deceived, Eve's desire ruled over the will of God. The three enemies of rulers are the three things she "fell" for: the deadly sins of the lust of the flesh, the lust of the eyes, and the pride of life. Scripture says that *"when the woman saw that the tree was **good for food**, that it was **pleasant to the eyes**, and a tree **desirable to make one wise** she took the fruit and ate."*[24] She saw the fruit was desirable and subjected mankind to its power when she exalted her desires above God's plan. After dominion was given over to satan, so went our desires *and* rulership!

But God promised that the situation would not remain this way forever. There was a promise of redemption. Eve was built and uniquely suited to help Adam accomplish the will of God. A woman, married or single, still holds that created destiny. The second announcement was that even with the advent of pain and sorrow, the child built within the body of the woman would destroy the works and power of the satan's dominion. God said to the tempter, *"I will put enmity between you and the woman, and between your seed and her Seed; He shall bruise your head, and you shall bruise His heel."*[25] Here, even in Eden, comes the first prophecy of a coming Messiah, the Seed of the woman, who would restore all things. War had been declared. The woman would be central to the attack.

## Jesus Christ, the "Last Adam," Came to Restore All Things

From the time of Eden onward, women came under the domination and subjugation of men in every culture and society, including that of ancient Israel. Although Israelite women generally enjoyed a higher status than did the women of pagan cultures, Hebrew society was a patriarchal society and Judaism was a patriarchal religion. Women were not eligible for the priesthood, and only men received a physical marker on their bodies—circumcision—as a sign of the covenant with God. After the temple was built in Jerusalem, women were limited to the outer "court of the women." Only men could proceed into the inner "court of the Jews," and only priests (who were all men) could enter the Holy Place to offer up the sacrifices. Only the high priest (also a man) could enter the Most Holy Place and then only once a year, on the Day of Atonement. But even in that day God was prophesying about a glorious day of His handmaidens to come. During the great harvest ingathering at the end of the year, huge lampstands were filled with holy oil and raised up to shine light on the city from the Court of Women. The Spirit of God is raising up His light among His women, vessels of His anointing, in this hour.

When Jesus appeared on the scene, many things began to change, including the status of women. Jesus seemed quite unconcerned about following social mores that excluded women from direct involvement in spiritual authority in public or in private, even in mixed settings. Just as He quietly overrode the interpretation of work allowed by the law and healed many on the Sabbath, He has overridden the regulations on women in ministry. The separation and restriction of women leading to their exclusion from public and private spiritual ministry is reflected in the developments of Judaism, the taproot and source of Christianity. There are many differences between modern and ancient Jewish custom just as there are many contradictions in the traditions of men and the ordination of God.

Most significantly, Jesus revealed Himself to women first after His resurrection and sent them to tell His other disciples that He had risen. Women, therefore became the first proclaimers of the risen Lord. In that day and culture the word of a woman was regarded as unreliable next to that of a man. For this reason women were not allowed to testify in court unless a man accompanied her who could corroborate her testimony. Yet all four gospels place the first news of the resurrection of Christ on the lips of women, corroborating the authenticity of the account and highlighting the significance of the event. Sending women as His personal eye-witnesses to the resurrection challenged age-old prejudices and firmly planted a standard, establishing women as spokespersons and witnesses to the works of God.

Jesus elevated the status of women to a higher place than at any other time since Eden. Paul called Jesus the "last Adam" who *"became a life-giving spirit"*[26] in whom *"all shall be made alive."*[27] First John 3:8 says that *"the Son of God was manifested* [to] *destroy the works of the devil."* This means that Jesus came to restore what satan destroyed or stole in Eden, including the place, authority and dominion, of women in equal partnership with men.

For centuries Eve's failure in Eden has been held out as an indicator of innate female moral weakness which, coupled with a misunderstanding of Peter's words about a man considering his own wife as the "weaker vessel,"[27] led to an erroneous conclusion that women are weak, inherently unspiritual and unable by means of creation to be equal to men. But in fact, even though created second, woman was created exactly equal to man and "a helper comparable" to Adam by comparison to all other creation.

## Two Tales of "Women's Liberation"

Women's liberation is not a modern, Western concept. What the Western world calls women's liberation is really a secularized and corrupted form that seeks to redress grievances through law. Jesus Christ has been liberating women for over 2,000 years, but He does it through inner transformation.

## Jacob's Well, Sychar, Samaria, c. A.D. 28

Remember the Samaritan woman whom Jesus met at Jacob's well outside the village of Sychar? (see John 4:1-42) This woman had such an ill reputation in town that she found it necessary to draw water during the hottest part of the day when no one else was around. One day, however, she approached the well to find Jesus resting there. Of course, she had no idea who He was. She must have been quite surprised when, contrary to all accepted custom, He spoke to her.

"Please give me a drink."

She scrutinized him for a moment through squinted eyes. "Why would you, a Jew, ask me, a Samaritan, for a drink of water?"

"If you only knew God's gift and who it is who has asked you this, you would ask Him and He would give you living water."

Seeing His empty hands and no bucket, she snorted softly. "And how would you draw out this 'living water'? This well is deep and you have no bucket. Do you think you are better than Jacob, our father, who dug this well centuries ago?"

The Man looked at her with eyes that seemed to bore right into her soul. She felt the urge to shrink back from His piercing gaze. "Whoever drinks this water," He said, pointing at the well, "will get thirsty again. Whoever drinks *My* water will never thirst again. Instead, My water will become in him a fountain that springs up to eternal life."

She looked at Him with a growing sense of uneasiness. Who was this man who was speaking to her of living water and eternal life? Suddenly, a tiny spark of hope ignited in her heart. "Sir," she asked softly, "please give me a drink of your water so I won't be thirsty or have to come to this well anymore."

The hint of a smile appeared on the Man's face as He said, "Go bring your husband."

She cast her eyes downward. "I don't have a husband."

"Quite right," He answered. "In fact, you have had five husbands and are now living with a man you are not married to."

Her head shot up in shock, and she felt blood rushing to her face. How did he...? How could he...? Now she was really starting to feel uncomfortable. She decided to change tack.

"Sir," she said with feigned calmness, "I see that you are a prophet. Tell me something; our fathers have always worshiped on this mountain, but you Jews say that Jerusalem is the only proper place to worship. Which is it?"

"The place of worship—whether on this mountain or in Jerusalem—is not as important as the attitude of worship. True worshipers worship the Father in spirit and truth. Those are the kind of worshipers the Father is looking for."

Not satisfied with His answer, she said, shrugging her shoulders, "Well, Messiah is coming someday, and He will explain everything."

A thrill of fear and awe and sudden joy shot through her as He looked her straight in the eye and said, "I am He."

Her eyes met His for one blazing moment. Her water pot dropped forgotten from her hands. She turned and dashed back into the village, calling out at the top of her voice. "Everybody, listen to me! Come here!"

Villagers poured out of their houses and shops at her cries. When they saw who it was, many turned away muttering and started to go back inside.

"Wait!" she cried. "Please wait! You've got to listen to me! You've got to come down to the well, all of you! There's a Man there who...who knows everything about me! He told me everything I've ever done! Could this Man be the Messiah?"

At this, everyone in the village rushed to the well to see for themselves. When they saw Jesus, many of them believed what the woman had told them. Excitedly, the people asked Jesus and

His disciples to stay with them. During the two days He was there, many more of the people in the village believed. Later, one of them told the woman, "Now we believe not just because of what you said, but because we have seen Him for ourselves and know that He is the Messiah."

This Samaritan woman is the first recorded person to proclaim Jesus as Messiah to the Gentiles and the first woman to proclaim Him at all. She witnessed of His nature and "preached" to the men of her village, and nowhere is there any hint that Jesus criticized her for such actions. On the contrary, nowhere do we find where Jesus ever forbids a woman to preach, teach or share the gospel.

### Oveira, near Kinshasa, Zaire, present day

Some years ago, Mahesh was holding evangelistic meetings in Kinshasa, Zaire. A woman, who was dying of gangrene poisoning and paralyzed from the waist down was brought across the river from Brazzaville to Kinshasa to the meeting. That night, lying on a stretcher in the midst of the crowd, she raised her hand and recited the sinner's prayer, receiving Jesus in her heart. At that moment, the healing power of the risen Christ went through her entire body and healed her of paralysis and gangrene. She jumped off the stretcher and started leaping up and down, giving thanks to God.

Several years later, Mahesh returned to the region, holding leaders meetings and evangelistic outreaches. On one day he took a brief tour of the fishing village of Oveira. As he was ministering among the poor at the river, a woman ran up to Mahesh, calling him "Papa." This woman, who was obviously well-known to all those around her, was the same dying, paralyzed woman who had traveled to Kinshasa for a miracle a few years earlier. She had received her drink of the living water that springs up to eternal life and, like the Samaritan woman at Jacob's well, had returned to her city bearing the good news of the Gospel. In the several years since, she had raised up an entire church and ministry in Oveira, with the Lord working mightily in signs and wonders the whole time.

She came for a drink and a healing; she received an ocean of inheritance, destiny, promise, anointing, and purpose for her life and the lives of others. God liberated one of His precious daughters. He released one of His mighty lionesses to roar—and people's lives were changed.

What Jesus did with the Samaritan woman of Sychar and the paralyzed (formerly!) woman of Oveira, He wants to do in the lives of all of God's daughters. He is the Lion of the tribe of Judah and He wants to restore their voices. The daughter of a lion is also a lion. The Lord wants to release all of His lionesses to roar once more and to once again assume their proper place of authority and dominion in His Kingdom!

## Endnotes

1. "Ethiopian Girl Reportedly Guarded by Lions," http://msnbc.msn.com/id/8305836.

2. Isaiah 11:6-9.

3. Romans 8:19-22.

4. Romans 8:14-18.

5. Revelation 5:5.

6. Romans 8:29.

7. Colossians 1:15.

8. Joel 2:28-29.

9. Luke 4:18-19.

10. Isaiah 61:2-4, 7, 10.

11. Hebrews 1:3

12. Genesis 1:27-28.

13. Genesis 2:18, 21-23.

14. John 14:16.

15. Isaiah 49:15.

16. Habakkuk 2:14

17. 1 Samuel 6:7,12 (NKJV).

18. I Samuel 16:7.

19. Discussion in this section adapted from Rebbetzin Tzipporah Heller, "Men and Women: A Jewish View on Gender Differences," http://www.aish.com/societywork/women/Men_and_Women_A _Jewish_View_on_Gender_Differences.asp.

20. Genesis 1:2 *The Five Books of Moses.*, trans. Everett Fox New York: Schocken Books, 1995.

21. Genesis 2:16b-17.

22. Genesis 3:1-7a.

23. Genesis 3:16.

24. Genesis 3:6.

25. Genesis 3:15.

26. 1 Corinthians 15:45.

27. 1 Corinthians 15:22.

28. 1 Peter 3:7.

# Chapter Two

# Woman: An Unfinished Journey

*"Binti wa simba na samba."*
—"The daughter of a lion is also a lion."

A woman made in the image of God and born again by His Spirit will be like the Lion of the tribe of Judah who made her. Her approach to life, the manner and means by which she deals with her identity, how she interacts with society, her response to life experiences and circumstances—all these will spring from the genetic replica of her Father in Heaven, an empowering fire from within. She was born for this, to reflect the glory and image of God. At least, she has been given that opportunity, capability, and destiny.

It is said that the great storytellers weave their tales in circles. The main characters of the story end up more or less in the same place where they began, except that in the end their lives and circumstances reflect the changes brought about by their reaction to their experiences along the way. Between the beginning and the end comes the great adventure, often a seemingly insurmountable challenge that appears to point to inevitable defeat or disaster. Then, just when all hope seems lost, something from deep within the hero or heroine, some quality of character or perseverance previously unknown, rises to meet and overcome the challenge, leading to triumph in the end. Sometimes the victory is clear and decisive, and everyone lives "happily ever after." But sometimes victory comes with the cost of realizing that the world has been changed in unalterable ways and the bittersweet awareness that some things will never be as they were before.

An example in literature is J.R.R. Tolkien's story about Bilbo the hobbit, whose very "hobbit-ness" makes him an unlikely candidate to ever venture forth from his comfortable hobbit-hole to go on a decidedly un-hobbit-like "adventure." Even so, he is chosen against his will for just such an adventure, and in the end the wisdom of that choice becomes clear. More than once he saves the day (and his companions) by drawing on strengths and qualities he never knew he had, yet were there all along. All it took were the right circumstances to bring them to the fore. Bilbo's destiny leads him beyond his simple image of himself as a domestic, home-loving, hearth-hugger to become at different times sage, warrior, enemy of himself, and beloved best friend of another. Eventually he returns home from his journey having discovered, more than anything else, *himself*. In the end, it is what he took with him from home that framed his journey.

Like Bilbo, a woman's identity is more than meets the eye. She is complex, individual and corporal, earthly and celestial. Every woman is an intricate figure somewhere between the fictitious "angel in the house" of Victorian domesticity and the real live Sojourner Truth, who was born into slavery and whose very name tells her story. Sojourner escaped her bonds and because of her relationship with Jesus became a powerful preacher, abolitionist and legendary women's suffragist. A sojourner in this life, she found the road to liberty, prepared for her by God before she was ever born. She led many others down that path from slavery to the truth of Christ. Her faith was unshakeable. In her most famous address on the issue of women's rights Sojourner said, "And ain't I woman? Look at me! Look at my arm! I have ploughed and planted, and gathered into barns...I could work as much and eat as much as a man—when I could get it—and bear the lash as well. And ain't I a woman?"

Sojourner Truth was a woman whose *voice* was *heard*. Uneducated and unsophisticated as she was, intellectuals, educators, politicians, doctors, lawyers, business executives, merchants, clergy—people from every walk of life and every trade and profession gave her their ear once she stepped into her destiny. They all witnessed the innate power, blazing passion and raw intelligence reflected in the voice of this former slave. Sojourner galvanized the anti-slavery movement of mid-19th-century America. She is a type for women today, journeying back to the Garden in search of the truth of their destiny, identity and voice according to the plan and intention of the Savior.

## The Power of a Woman's Voice

In a sense every woman is a Sojourner Truth. Her circumstances of life and birth may not reflect all that God has in mind. He is calling her to set her foot upon His pathway, the pathway to purpose and liberty: to find her calling, to find her place of influence and blessing for others; to find her voice. We see in Sojourner there is more to a woman's voice than the sound of her words. Nothing soothes the troubled or fearful heart of a child like the gentle, lilting words of a mother's lullaby. Even more so the "softness" in the sound of a woman's voice is also the perfect vehicle for weighty and powerful things the woman of God has to say. Women are innately connected to the spoken word. Her power to communicate aligns her with God who spoke the worlds into existence. All the more reason she should have governance over her influence upon others. Her voice is much more than sound. Through her speech the wisdom inherent in women enters her world and community.

The Torah says "ten measures of speech were given and women took nine of them." The complex combination of her intuition and intellect combine in what the ancients recognized as *sophia*. Wisdom is personified in Proverbs 8 as a woman: "*She takes her stand on the top of the hill, beside the way, where the paths meet. She cries out by the gates, at the entry of the city, at the entrance of the doors: 'To you, O men, I call and my voice is to the sons of men....listen, for I will speak of excellent things and the opening of my lips will come right things.*" Interestingly, Christ is revealed prophetically in the woman Wisdom in this chapter: "*The Lord possessed me at the beginning of His way, before His works of old. I have been established from everlasting, from the beginning, before there was ever an earth....Then I was there beside Him as a master craftsman; and I was daily His delight rejoicing always before Him.*"

This is a mystery, that in Christ were possessed the characteristics of woman in wisdom and power, as one called beside, rejoicing and working with God to do His awesome acts. These were that which God took out of Adam in the garden and built into His woman. In His death and resurrection, Christ reversed the curse and brought her back from the dead. In His resurrection, His body, one body of both male and female, is being raised up. The voice of Christ in the Woman of Proverbs is the voice being restored to the daughters of the Lion of Judah today. The Lion is on the move. He is roaring once again and this time He will not be silenced.

The woman's presence is unique and powerful when she is in harmony with the purposes of God in any situation. We see this in many powerful and moving stories that have emerged from the human drama and global tragedy of the Second World War. Stories of courage and honor and fortitude in the face of incredible hardship, brutality and horror. Stories of the triumph of the human spirit over the dehumanizing forces of ruthless tyranny. Stories so incredible and unlikely that they must be true because no one could make them up.

One of the most amazing comes out of the campaign in the Balkans of Eastern Europe. This region that contains the modern nations of Slovenia, Croatia, Bosnia, Herzegovina, Macedonia, Yugoslavia, Romania, Bulgaria, Albania, Greece, and Turkey endured some of the harshest and most brutal Nazi occupations of the war. The same region also produced some of the most intractable and fierce resistance fighting of any territories occupied by the Nazis. Ethnic and sectarian hatreds stretching back for centuries added to the volatile mix.

The brutality of the Nazi occupation was especially evident in the cruelties endured by innocent children. By victimizing the children, however, the Germans unknowingly unleashed a firestorm because they raised the fury of the mothers in the region. What could be more fearsome than the enraged voice of a woman defending her family and especially her children? Even more, the enraged voices of many women together? During the Nazi occupation these women banded together and became some of the fiercest guerilla fighters the Germans ever faced. They were dogged, determined, ruthless and seemingly unstoppable. They even developed a particular yell that they used when attacking at night. This yell was so fierce and bloodcurdling when screamed out in unison by a large chorus of women's voices that on more than one occasion it instilled such fear and terror into the hearts of German soldiers that they trembled in their boots, dropped their weapons and ran! The German occupiers also learned very quickly that these women guerillas were more ruthless in their treatment of the enemy than were many of the men.

Don't mess with a mother's children! She will rise up in fearsome wrath to defend her own! These women bring to mind the proverb, "*Let a man meet **a bear robbed of her cubs** rather than a fool in his folly.*"[1] *The Lord of the Rings* film version of J.R.R.

Tolkien's story of the war between good and evil presents a powerful prophetic image of the Spirit-filled woman of God—how she was created to be and how she is to be now, engaged in the battle for her seed. The princess Arwen, half-human and half being from another dimension, lays her life, personal well being and destiny on the line for love. To save the ringbearer, the young one who possesses the anointing to destroy the forces of evil, Arwen rides forth. In the film, young Frodo has been mortally wounded and his life is ebbing away as he quickly succumbs to the poison in his wound inflicted by a dark warrior. An accomplished equestrian, Arwen knows only her father can save Frodo. Finding him in the forest she tells him, "Hear my voice. Come back to the light." Protecting him with her body she rides to the river where through the power of her voice they will be saved. They are chased by a horde of dark Ring Wraiths, but Arwen is determined and unafraid as she fights to save the young one. Just escaping the Wraiths capture, she urges the white steed into the river. The Wraiths stop at the river's edge where they demand she give up the boy. Turning fiercely she faces them. "If you want him," she cries as she draws her sword from its scabbard, "Come and get him!" In her mother tongue, a language not of man, she begins to call upon the power of the river and the waters rise around her and Frodo. The flood rolls down the riverbed in great white forms of charging stallions much like the one Arwen rides. The evil ones are overcome as she prays. Laying down her own future that the young one be saved from the death creeping over him, her faith, her love, her devotion, purity, and fearlessness together with the power she possesses in the language that calls forth the river saves the ringbearer.

Like Miriam, Deborah, Mary, Sarah, and Hannah all in one, Arwen illustrates the invincibility of an anointed woman of God moving in the power of the Spirit to fulfill her destiny and serve His purposes in her generation. She is a mother in Israel, a woman who has a rich reward. This was the destiny of Eve before she used her own desire ahead of the desire of God. It is still the destiny of her daughters. Eve's name, *Chava*, means life. It is closely related to the Hebrew words for life, *chai*; *mechava* meaning to articulate or express; and *chevda*, joy. This powerful combination of life, expression and joy is the unique power of woman. Articulation of that expression is at the heart of the prophetic gift and is one of the reasons God uses women to prophesy.

## The Voice of the Bride

It is said that behind every great man stands a woman. That axiom has been around for a long time, but it is only in recent years that the true and significant influence of women on human history is being realized and in a large degree, appreciated. Although history provides many notable exceptions, women generally have exerted their influence on human affairs from the background, at least until the last two or three generations. While there is nothing ignoble about that, now it seems the Champion of our souls is bringing the hidden power of the woman to the forefront. Revealing His truth. Showing her glory. Restoring her to the purpose designed in the beginning. We hear her voice clearer and clearer as the final age unfolds.

The corporate voice of many women coming together in harmony in a joint cause and for a joint purpose releases great power. This is especially true in the spiritual realm, which is one reason why the powers of darkness fear the woman's voice and have worked so hard to silence it throughout the ages.

That silencing effort is part of the greatest story ever told. The epic story of God—His human creations, their "falling out," their struggle to survive, their climb back to fellowship and their redemption and ultimate reunification—is coming full circle. The journey that began with the very first man and woman in happy fellowship with God is returning home at last. Perhaps it is no coincidence that as the stage is set for the great last act before the final curtain comes down on this age, the eyes of all the nations are on Iraq, at the heart of the Middle East, a land in turmoil. For it was there, in the Land-of-Pleasure in the East[2]—in Eden—that we all began.

"At the beginning of God's creating...God created humankind in His image, in the image of God did He create it, male and female He created them." These are the words of God, penned by men who were "borne along by the Holy Spirit," revealing to us exactly what happened. In order to know where we are we must know where we have been. And the saga of the woman's voice is a significant part of that story.

Silencing the woman's voice was at the forefront of the enemy's strategy from the very beginning. The serpent deceived Eve, who then chose to disobey God's command, bringing Adam along with her. In the judgment that swiftly followed, God cursed the serpent and foretold pain, sorrow, and unsatisfied desire for Eve. Then it was Adam's turn.

> Then to Adam He said, "**Because you have heeded the voice of your wife**, and have eaten from the tree of which I commanded you, saying, 'You shall not eat of it': Cursed is the ground for your sake; in toil you shall eat of it all the days of your life. Both thorns and thistles it shall bring forth for you, and you shall eat the herb of the field. In the sweat of your face you shall eat bread till you return to the ground, for out of it you were taken; for dust you are, and to dust you shall return."[3]

Notice how God prefaced His judgment on Adam with the words: "Because you have heeded the voice of your wife..." Thus began a precedent of silencing and repressing the voice of women that has manifested itself in every generation and in every nation, culture and people group on earth. This is not to say that God ordained it so, but that it was the natural consequence of Eve's sin. Adam was wrong to heed Eve's voice not because she was a woman, but because at that time her voice and her heart were out of alignment with God's will.

Whether for good or for evil, there is power in the voice of woman. This is by God's design. That power was never rescinded after Eve's disobedience. As a result of her sin, her voice (and the voice of women collectively) became just as susceptible to the powers of darkness as to the Spirit of God. Of course, the man's voice is just as prone to corruption and evil as the woman's.

Throughout the Bible we find parallel accounts of the voices of women: voices used both for good and for evil along with the consequences of heeding or not heeding those voices. The Book of Proverbs contains repeated warnings to young men against the folly of listening to the words and enticements of adulteresses and prostitutes, voices which will lead them to destruction. Ahab, king of Israel, listened to the voice of his wife, the wicked and idolatrous Jezebel, and brought ruin and destruction upon himself and his kingdom. Job, to his everlasting credit, refused to heed the misguided counsel of his wife who told him to *"curse God and die."*[4]

On the positive side we find women like Deborah, whose voice conveyed wisdom in leading and delivering her people as a judge. Then there was Abigail. Her wise counsel was ignored by her worthless husband Nabal (his name means "worthless"), and he died as a result. David, however, heeded Abigail's words and was spared from committing sin in the passion of anger. Huldah was a respected prophetess whose advice King Josiah sought when he was setting out to reestablish God's law in the land. In the New Testament, Anna spoke prophetically to Mary and Joseph concerning their newborn son, Jesus. Priscilla, along with her husband Aquila, instructed the eloquent Apollos and *"explained to him the way of God more accurately."*[5]

In Sarai, Abram's wife, we see examples of both good and bad. God had promised Abram a son, but many years had passed and the promise remained unfulfilled. Sarai decided to help things along. She gave her handmaiden, Hagar, to Abram as a concubine. *"So Sarai said to Abram, 'See now, the Lord has restrained me from bearing children. Please, go in to my maid; perhaps I shall obtain children by her.'* **And Abram heeded the voice of Sarai.**"[6] Ishmael was born as a result of Abram's union with Hagar. By seeking to give Abram an heir by this means, Sarai went outside God's plan. So did Abram when he heeded the voice of his wife.

Later, after Isaac, the son of promise, was born, Sarah (Sarai's new name) insisted that her husband get rid of Hagar and Ishmael. *"Therefore she said to Abraham, 'Cast out this bondwoman and her son; for the son of this bondwoman shall not be heir with my son, namely with Isaac.'"*[7] This time, however, Abraham didn't want to go along. But God intervened. *"God said to Abraham, 'Do not let it be displeasing in your sight because of the lad or because of your bondwoman. Whatever Sarah has said to you,* **listen to her voice**; *for in Isaac your seed shall be called.'"*[8]

Why should Abraham listen to Sarah's voice this time when it was the wrong thing to do before? Because this time Sarah had realigned herself with the purpose of God. She chose faith over the power of the flesh to fulfill what God had spoken.

The silence of the voice of the Bride (woman) is a symptom and characteristic of life in a sin-desolate world. Restoration of the Bride's voice is the sign of the imminent advent of all things being made new. Jeremiah 7:34 says, *"Then* **I will cause to cease** *from the cities of Judah and from the streets of Jerusalem the voice of mirth and the voice of gladness, the voice of the bridegroom and the voice of the bride. For the* **land shall be desolate**". Compare this scene with that of the "new heaven" and "new earth":

*Now I saw a new heaven and a new earth, for the first heaven and the first earth had passed away. Also there was no more sea. Then I, John, saw the holy city, New Jerusalem, coming down out of heaven from God, prepared as a bride adorned for her husband. And I heard a loud voice from heaven saying, "Behold, the tabernacle of God is with men, and He will dwell with them, and they shall be His people. God Himself will be with them and be their God... And the Spirit and the bride say, "Come!" And let him who hears say, "Come!" And let him who thirsts come. Whoever desires, let him take the water of life freely.*[9]

The Lord is making all things new! The voice of the Bride is being restored!

## Jesus vs. Traditions of Man

This restoration will not happen without a fight −*"And I will put enmity between you and the woman..."*[10] Historically, women have been one of the main groups he has targeted for oppression. The spirit of anti-Christ has always been after the carrier of the Seed. Even Judaism, as it developed during and following the Babylonian Exile, came to be male-dominant and ultimately exclusive to men concerning spiritual privilege and power. The obligations placed upon males under Jewish law bore correlating responsibility and privilege. Those obligations included the requirements of prayers, study, and appearance in public worship throughout the day and throughout the year. It was a burden impossible for women to perform without neglecting or being absent from the great weight of responsibility required in ancient times to run a household and raise and train children. Mercifully, God relieved women of many of the religious obligations. Fathers, brothers, and husbands kept the commandments on behalf of the whole family or household. Ultimately traditions developed creating a spiritual culture wherein women were excluded rather than relieved. In time it left them as second class citizens with men assuming superiority through headship and privilege. The absence of women from spiritual settings, community leadership, and spiritual service gave way to inequality in educational development. The intention and command of Scripture evolved into complicated interpretations and innuendo separating the sexes in some way or the other in almost every walk of life and indicting the woman as possessing an inferior nature to man.

Rabbinical schools were on the rise during Jesus' day. They had ultimate influence on the Jewish culture. Scribes recorded the rabbis' sayings, known as the "oral law." Though not theoretically authoritative as the Scripture of written law, practically speaking, the sages' viewpoints and interpretations became more influential than Scripture in forming Jewish culture. There are countless examples throughout Jewish writings and traditions of male misperception of woman, negative assumptions upon her nature and role, and chauvinism relegating her outside levels of spiritual privilege and influence. We must remember that our Bible and our traditions have some influences from this root. Additionally many of the church fathers from the second century onward show themselves through their writings sadly prejudiced against the female constitution. Jewish rabbinical tradition came to regard the very voice of a woman, *kol b'isha erva*, as lewd. It was not to be heard by anyone but her own husband and certainly not to be sounded in the place or times of prayer lest it distract the men from praying and lead to sinful thoughts or actions. The fear of lewdness inspired by the presence of women led to the Great Rectification of Herod's temple in Jerusalem wherein a balcony was built to separate women from the festivities during the feast of Tabernacles.

The Talmud cites the sayings of Hillel: "the more women, the more witchcraft; the more maid—servants, the more lewdnessà"[11]

Jewish historian Josephus cites the Talmudic prohibition of women as witnesses in a court of law.

Tertullian, a second century church father whose influence in foundational theology is extensive, said of women, "Do you not know that you are each an Eve, you are the devil's gateway, you are the unsealer of the forbidden tree...You are the first deserter of divine law. You destroyed so easily God's image man, that on account of your guilt the Son of God had to die." Likewise Clement, a powerful church father who exercised signs, wonders, and miracles and was honorably mentioned by Paul in his letter to the Philippians[12] wrote, *"Man is stronger and purer since he is uncastrated and has a beard. On the other hand, women are weak, passive, castrated, and immature."* At the same time Clement extolled women martyrs in the ranks of the apostle Paul: "To these holy apostles were joined a very great number of others, who having through envy undergone, in like manner, many pains and torments, having left a glorious example for us. For this, not only men, but women, have been persecuted; having suffered very grievous and cruel punishments, have finished the course of their faith with firmness."[13] Before his conversion Paul had a hand in such persecutions. Non-Christian records such as Roman Governor Pliny's (A.D. 111-A.D. 113) letter to Emperor Trajan include references of women in church leadership roles such as "two female slaves who were called deaconesses."[14] Emperor Theodosius, followed Constantine. Zealous of promoting glory in the church he issued a law forbidding women entrance into the ministry if they had no children or were less than sixty years of age. Theodosius drew his conclusions from Paul's letters. Tertullian wrote in the 2nd century "It is not permitted for a woman to speak in the church [1 Cor 14:34–35], but neither [is it permitted her]àto offer, nor to claim to herself a lot in any manly function, not to say sacerdotal office."[15] Calvin, father of the Reformation, wrote, "Woman was created (after man) to be a kind of appendage to the man, on the express condition that she should be ready to obey him, thus God did not create two heads of equal standing, but added to the man a lesser help meet." These extreme prejudices have a spiritual influence behind them that is akin to racial prejudice. Let us remember that for centuries separation of persons for reason of their skin color was fully accepted and justified in religious teaching and practice. So it is with women.

We must take into account the influence of churchmen such as those mentioned who down through the ages have, by their authority, set doctrine and tradition which influenced the whole society. These seeds are still bearing fruit in circles where dead traditions over-ride the Presence and power of the Holy Spirit. We must remember that even Paul was trained by the ancient schools whose sages held prejudices against the power of a woman. Jewish born psychiatrist Karl Stern, a Roman Catholic, suggests there is extensive evidence that men as well as women in many cultures have been taught to be afraid of much of what is traditionally associated with the feminine. He shows the lives and influence of several contemporary thinkers of the modern age to support his proposition. He says this fear has influenced the influencers, primarily men according to tradition. It makes sense that deep gender bias generally accepted within a culture would tend to reproduce itself. Stern studied half a dozen primary influencers of the modern age and showed how their personal formation and worldview had dramatic effects on society's thinking in their generation and beyond. He believes there is a relationship between the evolution of science and development of social culture. He describes the conflict between the rational and the intuitive reflected in the scientific revolution of the past three centuries. Most notably in his book *Flight from Woman*, Stern encapsulates the affects of the fear of things female in the de-feminization and subsequent dehumanization of developing society. He also suggests, as does the new science of quantum theory, there is a hidden side, another face besides the rational one, to physical science just now being revealed. The hidden face is the intuitive one. The intuitive side of science is highly suggestive of the creation as revealed in Genesis when God spoke the worlds into existence, Christ rejoicing beside Him. The intuitive side belongs to the woman by nature. Stern writes, "If we equate the one-sidedly rational and technical with the masculine there arises the ghastly specter of a world impoverished of womanly values." Where does this fear of women's influence come from? It comes from the one who is afraid that given her place she and her seed will crush his power and authority completely. The enemy and deceiver made a determination in Eden to do everything to stop the revelation of the power of the woman.

In *Understanding the Trinity*, Alister McGrath writes about our developed knowledge and its relationship to our theology of God. "The point from which we have to look at something determines how much of it we can see," McGrath says. He uses the illustration of man understanding the moon according to the illuminated face seen from the earth. Yet there is an entire "dark side of the moon," an undiscovered face which no man has yet seen. We know it is there. We can assume certain things about what we do not see on the basis of what we do see. This is precisely the problem with the traditions and theologies that have developed regarding the woman. It is impossible for a whole perspective of the understanding of the woman to be placed within the doctrine and tradition of the church if the only perspective comes from men. The issue of womanhood in the church and the doctrines and traditions surrounding her are perhaps the most critically undeveloped of all other spiritual matters effecting society. To the degree that Christianity has "conquered" the ancient pagan world, particularly in the West, and has influenced the foundations of much modern society, in regards to woman our fundamentals are lacking. Prophetic utterance in vessels of earth is subject to the prophet. The prophet, to some degree, is the product and under the influence of the culture and fabric of his traditions until God breaks in with the "new thing" He has created. When Joel spoke about the future outpouring of the Spirit of God, he declared an essential change in the traditions of spiritual office. In his day there was no indication by practice, knowledge or tradition that gender, age, and station in life would be generally by-passed in selecting priests as God filled His community with His Rushing Breath. Jeremiah proclaimed a new thing in the earth wherein a woman would encompass a champion. The details were not given. Yet those declarations had their root in the ancient garden where woman was built in the glory of God. It is the responsibility of each generation to hear, declare, and model what the Sprit is saying. Looking to the beginning when God created woman in His image and likeness, there are indicators from which we may draw light and so adjust the strictures into which the woman has been thrust by sin and time.

Discussing the Trinity, McGrath says the clear view of the moon by an observer is proof of the existence of the unobserved side. While the absence of the dynamics to study the hidden part obstruct the possibility viewing it for the time being, the observer knows the hidden side is there. To understand things yet 'undiscovered' which are suggested but not fully revealed, McGrath points out the vital necessity of drawing a distinction between *kerygma* and *dogma*, proclamation and doctrine. Kerygma means the herald or proclamation of something. Kerygma in the Pauline letters of the New Testament are at the root of an essentially incompletely formed dogma on the power of the woman, particularly in church culture, but affecting her on a broader societal basis. Theologies evolved around women reflect their authors and the period in which they were developed. Additionally the enmity of satan toward the woman has had its impact. There are aspects of the truths of creation, the Logos, the dual natures of Christ, and the Trinity which indicate the hidden "mystery" contained in woman who was created as the archetype of the Bride of Christ. Dogmas on the Trinity and creation have much less influence on our views on woman than the references given by Paul in answer to conflicts over women's issues. The greater truths of God and Scripture support a much fuller inclusion of the woman than do the traditions we have generally followed. At the same time, in each fresh outpouring of the Spirit God seems to go right along playing by His own rules. Rules we find half revealed in the very beginning.

Proclamations taken from Paul's writings have effectively silenced, subjugated and hidden the power of the woman. But did the apostle intend or even say the same thing the tradition does? Did God? We think not. For while he seems to say woman should keep silent in the church, should not teach or hold authority but be subject to a husband, Paul writes to women as church leaders, sometimes naming them before the husbands with whom they served. Priscilla is mentioned together with her husband six times throughout Paul's letters. Three times Paul names her before her husband. In the culture of the day the first to be named in a letter usually held the higher authority than those named after. In a litany of co-laborers listed in Romans 16 Paul names many women prominently. They include Phoebe, a "deacon" at Cenchreae, the same word Paul used to describe men of that office in other letters to his son in the Lord, Timothy, and to the Philippians. The word in Greek translated as 'succourer' in the King James description of Phoebe is the word used for a legal protectorate in Roman culture and literally means to stand before in rank or to preside over. It is also another word for *helper*.

Paul calls Junias "notable among the apostles." Although King James' translators changed the original spelling to a masculine name (Junias), Junia was a woman's name in the time of Paul. There is no record of the name Junias at all. Church fathers Origen, Jerome, and John Chrysostom all hold the name to be that of a woman apostle. The latter wrote, "O! how great is the devotion of this woman, that she should be counted worthy of the appellation of apostle!" No commentator on the text until Aegidius of Rome (1245-1316) took the name to be masculine. Without commenting on his departure from previous commentators, Aegidius simply referred to the two persons mentioned in Romans 16:7 as *"these honorable men."*[16] That mention changed the woman Junia into a man in church kerygma and dogma from that time forward. Until these last days. Lydia mentioned was an influential business woman who was Paul's first convert in Philippi. She opened her home as a ministry center for Paul while he was in the region. He calls her a co-laborer with him to further the Gospel.[17] Chloe also hosted and likely oversaw a church in her home[18] as did many women converts of the day. Often coming to Christ first they then brought their families into the fold. Chloe's house church is mentioned in his letter to the church at large in Corinth. Mary, Tryphena, Tryphosa, Julia, Nereus' sister, and Rufus' mother are all mentioned by name by the apostle. These women make up a disproportionate number of the laborers in the harvest whom Paul mentions by name in his acknowledgements. It stands in direct opposition to the general assumption that Paul disallowed women in ministry!

Women were a vital part of the first century New Testament church. From deaconesses to fellow laborers and fellow prisoners in chains, Paul extols and names women as fully participating in the church and in the preaching of the gospel. In 1 Corinthians 16:16 Paul exhorts the church to *"submit yourselves to such as help and labor with us."* In the period immediately following the ministry of Paul and the apostles of Jesus, the church fathers wrote of men and women holding prophetic office, prophesying, speaking in tongues, practicing exorcism of demons and doing miracles in the church. Justin Martyr,[19] Eusebius[20] and Irenaeus[21] all wrote of these phenomena. Clearly during the days of outpouring experienced by Paul and for two centuries afterward both men and women held office in the church and moved powerfully in the Spirit both teaching and leading. They considered the human personality, much like a musical instrument made to sound by a plectrum, secondary to the invasion of the Spirit.[22] This is agreeable to Joel's proclamation that a day of liberation and equality was coming for men and women by the Spirit.

These examples must be added to the testimony and works of God throughout Scripture including His anointing of women as religious and national leaders in the Old Testament and Jesus' inclusion and association with women in the New Testament. The full spectrum of the apostle's writings must be taken into account to draw the right conclusion on his injunctions that seem to be against women. Doctrine concerning woman begins with her Creation in the image and likeness of God in the garden. In order for us to come to the destination God has marked out on His map, it is essential we start off at the right place. We must view woman before the fall, and receive her back through the cross of Christ and in light of the outpouring of the Holy Spirit beginning at Pentecost.

An understanding of the Trinitarian nature of God is essential to understanding the hidden power of the woman. We might ask how a woman, built differently from a man, is like God? A woman can be self sufficient to live and navigate, but that self sufficiency has been ordained to be interdependent, contributing to and receiving from a community of others beginning with her counterpart, man. Like her, man may be sufficient but not fully experiencing what was intended at creation until he is contributing and receiving from others in the community, beginning with woman. Humans are created to benefit and flourish for the sake of and in relation to others. This is love. This is also reflective of the Trinity who made man in His image. Possessing the ability to be and directing that ability from self to the edification and enjoyment of others, man glorifies God. God is love. As love reveals the Trinity love solves the conflict between kerygma and dogma on woman in our spiritual traditions. Beginning with love for one another, the Personas in the Trinity are self sufficient yet by the *will to power* (God's innate, sovereign authority), each is interdependent upon the other, submitting and deferring, upholding and enjoying. Each exists for the other and thereby makes the full expression of the individual image. This community of Personas is One, as the *shema* of Israel says, "The Lord our God is One." The specificity of individual expression of the different personas of God do not divide His unity, rather He exemplifies Himself by the Three being One. Each sufficiency exists not for its own primary sake but for the benefit of the other. Likewise female and male are one in Him. They share together in His fullness according to His creation, not according to their Fall. When God said, "It is not good for man to be alone" He was seeing Himself reflected in His creation. He said, "I will make a helper fit for him." Then God built a woman and they had a community.

Headship is a partnership. It is neither a situation whereby the women is the neck that turns the head or that she is one of two heads competing with one another. God has created them, male and female, to rule together. The two, equal, in harmony contributing to serve and fulfill the will of Him who is the Creator of the universe and Head of the church. Since Eden, under the influence of the one who holds ultimate enmity toward the woman, war has raged to silence and destroy woman made in God's image as man's perfect and effectual counterpart to do His will. The result of his influence has been a flight from woman; a supernatural corrupting fear, often twisting and using God's Word, to prevent allowing woman in.

In the Godhead, the Helper is a persona of God. So the woman "helper" is made in His image. The Holy Spirit is of the same substance and nature as the Father and the Son while exhibiting a different *Persona*. The Holy Spirit is sent from the Father and given by the Son. While exhibiting their power the

Spirit exercises His own. *"Not by might, not by power but by My Spirit, says the Lord."*[23] The Spirit is not dependent or independent. He is the Resident Lord of the Church, interdependent upon, and in love with Father and Son. Likewise the Father has handed all things to the Son. Yet the Son does nothing of Himself. This common unity, or community, of the Personas of God, His Community, helps us to understand God's intention for woman in relation to man. It should also help us to adjust and define our dogma on women.

Historically debate in the church has forced doctrinal clarification. Early theologians were uncertain as to whether the Holy Spirit was an activity, a creator, or God. It was not until nearly four hundred years after Pentecost that a council at Constantinople concluded the Holy Spirit is "the Lord and giver of life, who proceeds from the Father, and is worshipped and glorified with the Father and the Son." If the questions about a member of the God head, who is also the residing Lord in the church, were so incomplete and unsettled, the dogma on women were a long way from consideration. But now they have come to the forefront. Charismatic and fundamentalist theology today would find the mere suggestion that the Holy Spirit is less than God an absurdity. Still, while accepting the doctrine, church practice often denies the Spirit the place of power and authority of God. If equal to Father and Son, where is His authority in our traditions and practice? Where is His worship? Even suggesting the Holy Spirit be worshipped as God terrifies some traditionalists. If the Spirit performs functions that are specific to God, it follows He shares in the divine nature. Our theology, practice and prejudice toward the woman suffers similar inconsistencies. When God said of woman, "I will make a helper fit for him" He was showing that woman created, not as animals over whom man was given governorship, but in the image of God and made from the same stuff as man was of him, equal to him and to be a sharer in him.

Adam said, "This time she is it!"[24] Woman was sharer and partaker of the same nature of the man. She was ordained as a *parakletos*, one who is called into the empty place beside. Paul says, "Man was not made for the woman but woman was made for the man." Did he mean that woman was designed and built by God to please man and do man's will? There is no universal pattern in Scripture to support this. Man, male and female has been created in the image of God to do His will.

The traditional monocle lens of the maleness of God has produced a doctrine separating the genders in spiritual terms, making male apart from female to be a reflection of the image of God. While a man may be sufficient to be in himself, his sufficiency cannot reflect the fullness of the God community. Man was created to be interdependent with the persona of the likeness of God built into the woman. Such language makes some uneasy. Our traditions on women have lacked the image of the Trinity as a compass. Our dogma has not properly included understanding of creation. This has produced catastrophic vacuums in our understanding on women and their place of power in religious and secular culture. Those empty places have been filled by repression and rebellion. Throughout Scripture in times of strictest spiritual and cultural prejudice against women, God has abjectly ignored man's tradition and selected and empowered women as sovereign vessels of His Spirit to lead and direct His people. This should give us some clue. McGrath says of the Spirit, "A new experience of the reality and power of the Spirit has had a major impact upon the theological discussion of the person and work of the Holy Spirit." The same can be said of the use of women by God exemplified in dramatic occasions in history but now no longer a phenomena as much as common occurrence. The new experience of the reality and power of the Spirit being experienced by and manifest among women is having its impact upon church culture. It must be allowed to have its impact upon our theology as well. It is time to look again at the side of the moon we do see, and allow God to show us the other side, the side of the hidden power of the woman.

God made woman a perfect partner for man in order that together they might accomplish God's will. The will of a man and the will of the woman are illegitimate except they submit to the perfect will of God. A general devaluation of the feminine is the fruit of the old mindset that the purpose of a woman's life is to obey her husband. Obedience and submission are mutual functions of love. Lordship of sin over human desires coupled with lack of respect for the feminine gender has devalued woman. Abuse, pornography, infanticide, abortion, and chaos in sexual identity enforcing perversion including homosexuality are all affects of the devaluing of woman in light of thinking.

As man's equal counterpart, together, the man and the woman were to have dominion. This part of creation theology is widely agreed upon. However, the woman's failure to recognize satan's seduction and her obedience to his will according to her own desire is still seen by many to have never been fully dealt with at Calvary. Generally this reservation stems from Paul's writings about the submission of women in light of Eve's transgression. The word for woman is also the word for a married wife. Read in that context there is no support for traditions making the female gender secondary to the male gender. Made of the same substance, woman was given a body and a persona to unite in communion as one with the man that by her they might be complete and multiply in love to fill the earth over which they had been made governor.

In his letters to the churches and to his disciple Timothy, the apostle Paul addresses several of the points that most concern women. The edicts of silence and submission that have summarily changed the history of women in the church through Paul's writings must be reviewed in full light. If Paul meant for all women to keep silent in all churches, his teaching about the gifts of the Spirit are invalid. If he meant that no woman should hold authority in the face of men God contradicts Himself by His own history of using women to prophesy and lead. Consider the time and culture in which Paul lived and wrote. Women were introduced to the liberty and power of the Spirit. Many of them were uneducated and unaccustomed to having liberty to speak and ask questions of male authority in public. In first-century synagogues it was permissible and customary to interrupt the preacher to ask questions. A sermon followed the reading of Scripture. The sermon was more of a lesson and congregants were encouraged to ask questions. The rabbinic teaching method was for the rabbi to seat himself (like in the story of Martha and Mary) and wait until someone asked a question.

The most practical suggestion to maintain a most edifying gathering was for those women to listen and learn and take their discussions home. Imagine the husbands whose spiritual and natural communication with their own wives was suddenly dramatically enriched. Even the sound of religious settings changed with Christ and Pentecost. The woman's voice, once considered a temptation in religious settings, was suddenly heard in those same settings! Imagine the potential for offense and debate everywhere men and women gathered for worship.

In addition to adjusting the Jewish traditions to the outpouring of the Sprit and fulfillment of prophetic Scripture, the church was contending with pagan cults such as those of Ephesus and Corinth. Heresies and fables abounded. In Ephesus, the Temple of Artemis was the central influence of religion and culture. The goddess Artemis was believed to protect women during childbirth, an issue Paul mentions in his letters. The cult taught that the first human was a woman. Born before her brother, the doctrine of Artemis gave women spiritual authority over men. Paul reminded the church that Adam was created and then God built the woman out of his side. Paul went on to add that neither man or women is superior to or independent of one another. He referred everyone back to Eden for clarity.

Judaism holds almost universally that the first human, *adam*, was androgenous—that is male and female characteristics reflecting God fully—dwelt together in one person. God put the human into a deep sleep and separated out that which was female and built a woman. The two became one again in marriage, sharing and completing one another to fill the earth and have dominion over it according to God's command. This state of perfection was marred when Eve subjected herself to desires of the eyes, heart, and mind which, contemplating the fruit and being deceived by her own desires were contrary to the desire and command of God. The entrance of sin marred the perfection of creation. With sin came separation from God and from her other half. God told her, "Your desire shall be for (the man) and he shall rule over you." This was not a command. It was a foretelling of the fate befalling her mistake. But like His word to Cain concerning the sin which desired to rule over him, woman can master the power of sin through Christ and walk in full restoration to her original place of power. Whether the first human was both male in female in one body or not, we know that God fully had woman in mind when He made the first human. His creation was not complete or worthy to be called 'very good' until He had set woman in it as a crowning jewel to show forth His glory. Christ, the Champion of God and the Seed of the woman who would crush enmity's head, has come. He has purposed that woman be received back in to the place ordained for her before corruption came. His body will be both male and female as one, holding Him as Head over all. In describing the Trinity, Augustine used the metaphors of rays to sun, the ray being the radiant outshining of the sun. He also used the analogy of a river in relation to its source. In the same way, woman is the glory of man, the ray to the sun or the river to the source in the way that the Spirit is to the Father and the Son. How can we prescribe either a secondary nature or secondary place to her?

Jewish society had always been patriarchal, oriented toward the male as the principal spiritual burden bearer. Adam, the son of God, was not deceived but knew what he was doing when Eve brought him the forbidden fruit, and he ate knowing of his sin. Thus the man became the principle burden bearer for the sin of the first family. Judaism's male orientation stems from this responsibility. But the obligations became privileges exclusive of woman. Unable to save himself, the burden bearer Adam need-ed a Savior to redeem his family from sin and the curse. Christ came, the firstborn, the Son, the Burden Bearer according to Isaiah. Having prepared a body for Himself in which He would bear the burden of sin and redeem the creation of God, *"Surely he has born our transgressions and carried our sorrows...and by His stripes we were healed...the Lord has laid on him the iniquity of us all."*[25] The patriarchy of Judaism enforces the emphasis on the firstborn son as the "redeemer" of the family. Inheritance was passed through the male children or next male relative. Interestingly, proof of one's Jewish genes and citizenship in Israel is established through a man's mother not through his father.

The religious practices and their influence upon the whole culture arising in Judaism during the centuries before the birth of Jesus solidified the diminishing role and influence of the woman upon society. Even Scripture was interpreted by the sages to be against her. For example the passage from Exodus 20:17, *"You shall not covet your neighbor's house; you shall not covet your neighbor's wife, nor his male servant, nor his ox, nor his don-key, nor anything that is your neighbor's."* Obviously the point of this command is that one should avoid all forms of covetousness. But because the wife is listed among slaves and property, woman was eventually seen as being equivalent to the slaves and posses-sions of her husband. A far cry from what God said. Women became second-class citizens looked upon as having an inferior nature prone to sin, deception, moral weakness and a tendency to influence others to sin. All because of what took place in Eden and the added twisting of Scripture.

It is worthwhile also to remember that Corinth and Ephesus, the cities that were home to the recipients of Paul's letters containing his words on women, were centers of pagan cult worship. Various aspects of the answers he gave suggest the questions posed to him may have come from problems arising from pagan cultural influence or heresies in the church. Paul wrote *"that you might charge some that they teach no other doctrine, neither give heed to fables and endless genealogies, which minister questions, rather than godly edifying which is in faith."* Judaism and the pagan religions were infused with fables and endless genealogies. Perhaps Paul referred to a section of the Talmud when he said women should keep silent in the churches and be in submission as the Torah says: "All are qualified to be among the seven [who read publicly from the Torah in the synagogue on the Sabbath], even a minor or a woman; however, the sages ruled that a woman should not read from the Torah out of respect for the congregation." Indeed it was a "disgrace" in Jewish religious tradition. But the oral law of rabbinic tradition, not the written one of God, commanded it.

Although there are traditions in the Mishnah that claim to go back to the days of the Great Assembly in the days of Nehemiah (5 B.C.) and a few as late as A.D. 3, the main body of teachings is attributed to sages from the middle of the first century, through to the second decade of the third century A.D. Paul was trained in the rabbinical traditions which produced the Mishnah. Judaism developed very strong and forthright teachings concerning ni·DAH that exceeded the command or practicality of the Torah. The Mishnah compares the impurity of a menstruating woman to that of the uncleanness of an idol.[26] According to the oral traditions preserved in the Mishnah, failure to heed laws concerning menstruation was considered one of three transgressions that would cause women to die in childbirth. In his letter to Timothy the apostle makes what is likely a reference to the oral tradition when he says, *"Notwithstanding she shall be saved in childbearing, if they continue in faith and charity and holiness with sobriety."*

Jesus displayed God's lack of spiritual and cultural prejudice against women. His behavior confronted and violated entrenched religious and social traditions. The spiritual and natural presence and power of the woman extended beyond childhood and home in Jesus' life. His mother was the encapsulation of the prophecy of God to satan *"her seed shall crush your head."* God entrusted the very life of His only begotten Son to the body, mind, and desire of a teenage woman. Mary was a "new Eve", *chava*, mother of all the living. Unlike her predecessor, Mary said, *"Be it unto me according to Your word."* She surrounded a Champion and trained His hands for war. Elizabeth was filled with the Holy Spirit and became the first person, man or woman, to bless and prophecy over Jesus while He was still in the womb. The prophetess Anna was one of two witnesses to the Consolation of Israel when He was presented as a babe to the Lord in the Temple. The first miracle Jesus performed was at the behest of a woman. Already considered a spiritual leader and claiming to only do what He saw His Father doing, Jesus obeyed the command of Mary at a prominent community event. The first Gentile Jesus ministered to was a woman in Samaria. He spoke to her publicly, a taboo because of her gender and ethnicity, and He sent her as His first evangelist. He even asked to drink out of her cup! The first persons to witness His resurrection were sent by Him to testify to His other disciples. Those first witnesses were all women.

Jesus welcomed women into the ranks of His followers, not as tag-alongs but as students and disciples. In Luke 10:38-42. Jesus is teaching in the home of Mary and Martha. While Martha is performing her womanly duties, her sister takes a place sitting sat the feet of the Rabbi, not the customary place for a woman who was to receive the rabbi's instructions through her husband at home. Martha points out that she is bearing the woman's burden alone and asks Jesus to back her up by sending Mary to help her serve. But He rebuked Martha instead. In so doing, He rebuked the culture that excluded women from spiritual instruction because of their obligations at home. In those days sitting at the feet of a teacher was interactive. Synagogue, from which early church tradition developed, was more question and answer than one man preaching a sermon to many quiet observers. Therefore, we can assume Martha overheard her sister's voice, intermingled with the men's asking Jesus to explain the Kingdom of God. Most of us have had the experience of uncomfortable distraction when persons depart from the norm of our cultural comfort zones. Busy, religious Martha stepped in to conform her sister's embarrassing display to the accepted cultural and religious practice of the day. Imagine her consternation, and that of those in the house, when He said, *"Martha, Martha, you are worried and troubled about many things. But one thing is needed, and Mary has chosen that good part, which will not be taken away from her."*[27] Her spiritual inheritance was to join the men as a disciple. It was an inheritance given by the Lord which would not be taken away.

Jewish men began each day with the prayer, "I thank You, Lord, that I was not born a Gentile or a woman." Though some suggest that the prayer is a complicated expression of the obligation and thus the privilege of a man in bearing more responsibility towards the community than a woman does, it is more often prayed with prejudice than honor toward the "weaker vessel." A woman's place was in the home. In the home her voice was subject to that of her husband. To the (male) Jewish mind, women were morally, intellectually and legally inept. At the same time, the biblical evidence of women of wisdom and influence such as Miriam, Sarah, Deborah, Abigail, Huldah, Elizabeth, the Mary's, and many others clearly shows us that

God never held this prejudice. He has been on hand throughout history to pour out His Spirit upon women as well as men. In the power of the anointing and through gifts of prophecy they have lead, protected, instructed and preserved His people. Her place in the home is an indicator of the authority and influence ordained for her in the residence of God, the church which is His dwelling among His family.

It was tradition-busting practices such as these that got Jesus into trouble with the Jewish religious leaders. More than once they accused Him of violating—and therefore destroying—the Jewish law. Jesus' response was just the opposite: "*Do not think that I came to destroy the Law or the Prophets. I did not come to destroy but to fulfill. For assuredly, I say to you, till heaven and earth pass away, one jot or one tittle will by no means pass from the law till all is fulfilled.*"[28] Everything Jesus did was to *fulfill* the law, not destroy it. This included treating women as the mental and spiritual equals of men and welcoming them into the ranks as His disciples and students of the Word of God, as well as making them legal witness of His claims and messengers of His Kingdom.

By Jesus' day the Torah, the original body of law handed down by God through Moses, had been embellished by over 600 manmade conditions, restrictions and rabbinic interpretations. Intended originally to "protect" the Torah and to help ensure that no one violated it, these embellishments, called the Talmud, came to be regarded just as binding and authoritative as the Torah itself. Instead of freeing the people from the fear of breaking God's law, however, the Talmud added a much heavier legalistic burden for them to bear. The Christian traditions regarding women are no different. Jesus came to fulfill the Torah—God's *law*—not the Talmud—man's additions. Jesus came to destroy the works and the yokes of the devil, including the well-entrenched traditions of man that were out of order with the Word of God. This work continues today by the Holy Spirit and in this hour is particularly focused on the restoration of the woman to her spiritual destiny.

After the prophecies of Malachi, the biblical record of the Voice, *bat kol*, the gift of prophecy, was silent for nearly four hundred years. While performing his service in the temple, Zecharias, the father of John the Baptist, experienced the Voice of the Lord accompanied with a miraculous sign. The miracle was the loss of the priest Zecharias' voice until the prophecy he was given produced a second miracle, conception in barren Elizabeth's womb. After four hundred years of silence from Heaven, this event was a sign to all. The gift of prophecy, called in Hebrew *the daughter's voice*, accompanied with miraculous signs was the uncontested Voice of the Lord. These two witnesses, the Word and the miraculous works, were held to be uncontestable evidence that God was speaking. This is the foundation for Jesus' repetitive emphasis on hear and see, do and say. The testimony of signs accompanying the messenger's words indicated God was with him or her. The prophetess Deborah carried this anointing as the stars and the river moved to assist the victory she prophesied. But tradition killed man's ability to hear what the Spirit was saying. Turning to trust in the arm of the flesh often gave way to reckless judgment and rejection of the messenger God sent. Through Zecharias and Elizabeth, the Voice of the Lord in prophecy and the miraculous had returned to Israel, preparing the way for the Lord. Soon after, Simeon and Anna prophesied over the babe Jesus. The babe Himself was a sign accompanying the word delivered through Gabriel. Conceived without a man; born of the Spirit by the woman God chose.

Concurrent with the four hundred silent years the rabbinical schools arose. The oral traditions attempted to fill the void with an assurance of God's continuing presence among His people. But as happens when man attempts to provide the strength of the flesh as a substitute for the power of the Spirit, the fruit turned to bitterness.

Those present when Jesus was baptized by His cousin John in the Jordan experienced the Voice of the Lord when they both heard and saw. The Voice said, *"This is My beloved Son, in whom I am well pleased."* The Holy Spirit descended from Heaven in the form of a dove and rested upon Christ.[29] Some present both saw and heard the Voice. The event was tantamount to Moses on Sinai. This twofold Voice was to become the trademark of Christ's ministry on earth. His words were accompanied consistently by miracles attesting to their authority as being from Heaven.

But it was that Voice some disciples of the rabbinical schools of Jesus' day often rejected and persecuted. One of those disciples was the man whom Jesus' met on the road to Damascus. In a vision Saul was confronted by the Voice. *"Saul, Saul, why are you persecuting Me?"* A sign accompanied the Voice, who called Himself Jesus. Like Zechariah temporarily lost his voice, Saul temporarily lost his sight. Was God trying to get a message to the religious order of the day that things interpreted the way they had previously seen and heard them to be were about to change? Tradition, particularly religious tradition is one of the hardest things to kill. The conflict between God and religion is an age-old one. Finding his own 'voice' a fair replacement, the religious man will excuse himself from otherwise hearing and obeying the Voice of God.

Like the story of the women with the issue of blood no doctor but Jesus could heal, the church is hemorrhaging because of the women's issue. More than one half of God's end-time army has been immobilized because of bad theology and fear of man. It is time for her to reach out and touch the tzitzith, the knotted fringes of prayer and revelation on the garment of the Anointed One. He has come to heal her and end the uncleanness of her days of separation.

## Have We not Mothers to Whom We Have Listened?

Like Jesus, nearly all of us have been shaped, instructed, and influenced by a woman: our mother. A contradiction stands in bold opposition to patriarchal 'fatherhood theology' that has relegated woman to the kitchen. There can be no father without a woman equally involved! A man cannot become a father unless a mother is in full agreement giving conception and nurture to the seed he brings. To assume she has no authority to contribute her influence to the growth and admonition of the child produced is contrary to nature. Yet that is exactly what religious tradition has done with much of the woman's God-given place in the formation of society, beginning in the church.

This is true in the spiritual realm as well as it is in the natural and physical. In Hebrew Old Testament, the Voice, the Glory and the Wisdom of God, are all *feminine* word forms. Communication, particularly speech, is our primary means of influence. By speaking we enhance our relationships and encourage growth and change. Communication is the natural tendency of woman. She tends to constantly contribute by communication with those around her. But her influence is only as powerful as she is allowed in. By comparison, men tend toward the opposite. The nature of men is more silent and prone toward isolation or individualism. The feminine quality of communication builds community. Family and the Godhead have this in common.

Allowing woman in to her place will build society and build the church into a more productive and powerful community. See how male and female ruling together become productive, more productive than either one alone. Throughout most of Israel's history, and in the church, focus upon the male attributes of fatherhood and manhood attributed maleness to God. Particularly in matters of power the feminine has been excluded. We must accept that the woman was made in the image of God.

The unique strengths innate to woman are found in Him. The projection of almost complete maleness upon God has led to traditions that attribute leadership almost exclusively to men and prohibit women from leading. This prejudice against the feminine has contributed to the exclusion of the Holy Spirit—the power of God and the primary agent of redemptive restoration for all—from much of our religious culture. We have discussed the similarities between the nature and work of the Holy Spirit to the strengths and characteristics of the woman. When we fully welcome the Holy Spirit we can fully welcome woman. And perhaps the converse is true. At the very least, by observing the Holy Spirit at work in the "community" of the Godhead, we can get a glimpse of God's plan for woman. The Spirit is the "bond of love," as Augustine said, equal in every way to the Father and the Son.[30] The Holy Spirit is called "the power of God."

Wherever the Spirit of God works, He breaks bondages and releases people into the liberty and light of the Gospel of Jesus Christ. One of the common signs of this new spiritual liberty is the re-emergence of the voice and power of women. As it was in the first coming after those many years of silence, from Anna in the temple to Mary at the garden tomb, with the advent of His second coming, some of God's greatest instruments will be women. It is God's destiny and desire to release women in their end-time calling and ministry. The Lord is going to use women as well as men as those who make up the great company proclaiming His word. God is releasing the daughters of the Lion and they will roar and take the prey.

## The Church: Body of Christ, Bride of Christ

When Christ died at Calvary He fulfilled the law. His death satisfied the law's righteous demand for judgment on the sin of mankind. With the law's demand satisfied, the way was open for a new covenant, a covenant of grace sealed with the blood of Jesus. Now anyone anywhere could come to God by way of the

Cross, have his or her sins forgiven and receive eternal life. This body of believers of any and every age and generation constitutes the Church, the Body of Christ in the world, which He established and ordained to bear testimony of Him before the world and to carry His message of salvation to the nations.

The New Testament also depicts the Church as the Bride of Christ, being beautified and prepared for His arrival as the divine Bridegroom. This image, more than any other, brings out the presence and importance of the feminine aspect of the Church. Body and Bride together speak of a great and diverse company of saints, the fullness of God's sons and daughters.

Biblical, historical and archeological evidence reveal more and more that in the earliest days of the church, women worked and served on essentially equal terms with men. Women taught, evangelized, established and led house-churches, provided financial support, and generally were actively and significantly involved in every other aspect of church life. There is also biblical evidence that women functioned in diaconal and even apostolic capacities.

Women were a major presence in the early church. And, in fact, history and archaeology bear this out. From the beginning, Christianity proved to be extremely appealing to women, in part, at least, because of the high degree of respect and status it afforded them as people. Rodney Stark, a sociologist who has done extensive study on the rise of Christianity from a sociological standpoint, writes, "Christianity was unusually appealing because within the Christian subculture women enjoyed a far higher status than did women in the Greco-Roman world at large."[31]

Compared to the pagan culture of the Roman Empire which devalued women and consigned them to a second-class and distinctly inferior status, coming into the Christian culture was, for women in particular, like coming from the darkness into the light. It was also like coming from death to life, not just spiritually but also socially and culturally.

Christianity valued rather than exploited the hidden power of the woman. For the descendants of Eve, the life-giver, early Christianity's culture of life empowered women spiritually and released her to fulfill her destiny to nurture and shape the nascent church. In a world where infanticide, particularly of female babies, was widely practiced, the church valued girl infants as highly as boys. Amidst a morally decadent society that devalued human life in general, Christianity forbade abortion and marital infidelity, encouraged virginity before marriage in both males and females and took great care to look after widows and orphans. Many of these ministries were natural provinces for women because of their innate nurturing nature.

Unlike the predominant pagan society, which often married off its daughters as early as age twelve, usually in arranged marriages, the church strongly discouraged both practices. Christian females were not married off as children and were not forced to marry against their will. Consequently, Christian women generally married later than their pagan counterparts and had more voice as to whom and when they married. With greater opportunities to enjoy their freedom and to mature experientially before marriage, Christian women had a wider reserve of time to help others in need and, consequently, were instrumental—even vital—to the formation of a supportive and tightly knit Christian community that gave the emerging church more power than the mighty sword in winning over the Empire.

Ancient and modern sources agree that even in its earliest days, conversion to Christianity was far more prevalent among females than among males. This has indeed been true throughout history. In every generation, women have outnumbered men as active believers, members, worshipers and servants in the church, often by significant margins. Does it make any sense, then, that God would deliberately and by design effectively silence half or more of His "army" by restricting them from positions of leadership, influence, and public prophetic witness?

## An Unfinished Journey

In many ways, the original revelation of the kingdom of God was as a woman's world! The advent of the Third Person of the Godhead moved woman from third class to first. And, in its earliest years, it appeared that the church was working out that revelation in flesh and blood on earth. Women had found their place! Eve's voice was being restored! God's lionesses were roaring again!

But it was not to last. Within one or two generations after the passing of the apostles, the traditional male stance reasserted itself and severely repressed the voice and authority of women in the church. Eve was silenced once again. The enemy's deception in the Garden, thought dead and defeated at the cross, proved more resilient than ever. For nearly 2,000 years, with a few notable exceptions, women in the church, by and large, have been denied the opportunity to enter into their full God-given destiny.

Things *are* beginning to change, however. God's purpose will win out. Women, particularly Christian women, are on an unfinished journey. Like Bilbo in the midst of his adventures, Christian women are still in the process of discovering who they are and where they belong. The journey is still in progress, but the end is in sight! Ahead on the horizon is the misty form of our destination: a church where women as well as men enter into their full inheritance and destiny as sons and daughters of God, united in purpose, equal in authority and sharing a common future of fulfilled potential in the eternal Kingdom of our heavenly Father! Eve is returning to Eden, arriving back at the origin of her purpose and stepping onto the path for which she was created.

As women in pursuit of God's purpose and our destiny in Him, we are in good company. Join me now, as we look at the lives of four biblical women whose experiences represent our own quest for our full identity and voice in the Kingdom of God. We will begin with Rahab of Jericho who, against the certainty of death in her native culture, grasped at the chance of life in the culture of God's people—and claimed her inheritance.

## Endnotes

1. Proverbs 17:12.
2. Schocken Bible: Volume 1 *The Five Books of Moses*, Everett Fox.
3. Genesis 3:17-19.
4. Job 2:9.
5. Acts 18:26b.
6. Genesis 16:2.
7. Genesis 21:10.
8. Genesis 21:12.
9. Revelation 21:1-3; 22:17.
10. Genesis 3:15.
11. Tractate Abot ch. 11.5. *Hillel, sayings of.*
12. Philippians 4:3.
13. Clement *ad Cor.* c. v. vi. Abp. Wake's translation.
14. Pliny, Epistle 97.
15. *The Veiling of Virgins* 9 [A.D. 206].
16. Viri. 9.
17. Acts 16.
18. 1 Corinthians 1:11.
19. Justin Martyr, *Dialogue* 82, 87, 88. *Apology* 2:6.
20. A. Stepahnou "*The Charismata in the Early Church Fathers*" Greek Theological Review 21, Summer 1976.
21. Irenaeus *Haer* 3:11; 5:6; Ap Pred 99.
22. Athenagoras *Legat* 7; *Chortatio ad Gracecos* 8; cf. Dodds, p.64 and n. 2; DeSoyres, pp. 66—68.
23. Zechariah 4:6.

24. Fox, *Five Books of Moses* translation from original Hebrew.

25. Isaiah 53:4-6.

26. Shabbat 9:1.

27. Luke 10:41-42.

28. Matthew 5:17-18.

29. Matthew 3:16-17.

30. Alister E. McGrath, *Christian Theology An Introduction*, third edition, Oxford University, Blackwell Publishing, 313.

31. Rodney Stark, *The Rise of Christianity*, (San Francisco: HarperSanFrancisco, an imprint of HarperCollinsPublishers, 1996), 95.

# Part Two

## The Hidden Power of a Woman's Faith

*The body's filth cannot touch the pure soul, and snow-drifts cannot destroy living seeds. This life is but a threshing floor of sorrows in which souls have their adversities sifted out before they give their yield.*

—Kahlil Gibran

# Chapter Three

# Rahab:
## A Different Spirit

Because one woman dared to believe, moreover dared to follow her faith with deeds, something unimaginable, something historic, something impossible happened.

> *But it came to pass on the seventh day that they rose early, about the dawning of the day, and marched around the city seven times in the same manner. On that day only they marched around the city seven times. And the seventh time it happened, when the priests blew the trumpets, that Joshua said to the people: "Shout, for the Lord has given you the city! Now the city shall be doomed by the Lord to destruction, it and all who are in it. Only Rahab the harlot shall live, she and all who are with her in the house, because she hid the messengers that we sent."*[1]

"My life in exchange for yours...and that of my family as well." Guarded and hopeful, their host spoke in low, hurried tones. "Deliver us as we have heard your God delivered you from Egypt and we shall serve Him!"

The small strong hand that tightly clasped the hand of Judah's prince, and the dark eyes that gripped his eyes even tighter, belonged to a Canaanite. A woman. And a harlot. In these violent, terrible times few persons possessed their lives—much less their own bodies—as their own. Here in Jericho, as in Egypt, part of the culture's "hospitality" was extended by means of the city's *khans*, inns such as Rahab's.

Upon entering the city under the pretense of buying stores and seeking passage among one of the northern-going caravans, the two Israelite spies had inquired about lodging. They had been directed to this particular *khan*. It had proven to be a good choice. No request of theirs had been refused. Rahab had dutifully extended Jericho's hospitality, and thus the protection of King Keret, as could be expected. Now, her palm pressed against Salmon's, Rahab's pulse kept rhythm with his own—*teh-thump-teh thump-teh thump*—as if the very force of their lives had been calculated to converge like a pair of the wild gazelles that lapped at Jordan's edge in the predawn mists every morning. Destiny had come calling.

Sitting on a fat oasis in the Jordan Valley nearly 1,000 feet below sea level, Jericho was the most powerful and most strategic of any of the city-states to the north and west. Above it lay Ai, whose king paid uneasy tribute to Keret in order to maintain the balance of power between the two sovereigns. If Jericho toppled, the security of the whole region would be compromised, leaving it vulnerable to any taker. Like the city itself, Jericho's king bore the name of the most revered deity of Canaan, honoring the god who had given the city into his father's hand. Keret's army protected not only Jericho's four thousand inhabitants but also the residents of several tiny outlying villages that in times of danger sought shelter in the shade of Jericho's palms. City and villages alike irrigated their fields and slaked their thirst from the abundant and unfailing spring that fed the oasis—one of the main reasons for Jericho's strategic importance.

This perennial water source was the prize of the region. Many were the envious eyes that had beheld this oasis and the city that guarded it, coveting their possession. In the very shadow of Jericho's massive walls slave and serf labored with scythe and hoe, tilling and sowing the mineral-rich soil nourished by the spring. As a backdrop to this pastoral scene, Jericho's 26-foot-tall circular stone tower stood guard over all, its watchmen ever alert and vigilant. It pierced the sky amid graceful palms that stood both within and without the 15-foot-high double stone wall that encircled the 10-acre interior settlement. Keret had built the mound of Jericho into a legendary, impenetrable defense. During the reign of this ruthless god-king, the City of Palms had never been assaulted successfully. Every attempt at seizure had failed.

In addition to the rich vegetation wrapping the "jewel of the Jordan" in luxuriant green, there were within easy reach mineral fields from which salt was gleaned. This prized preservative, together with the highly sought linen cloth *byssus*, spun from flax, was the heart of the local economy and drove the trade routes between Canaan and Egypt of which Jericho and her king were the gatekeepers.

Each spring the offerings and vows presented in worship at the great Moon Festival assured fertile produce from those fields whirling out beyond the city's walls like the skirts of a dancing girl. Keret sowed and the earth gave up her yield. The field hands only imitated the god as they toiled along the flaxen furrows from the first light of day until dusk's curtain dimmed the light beyond a man's ability to see his blackened hands.

Few of Jericho's subjects ever saw the interior of Keret's residence. Rumor held that booty from his former conquests gilded his private quarters in luxurious opulence—a far cry from the rest of the city's residents, who lived in the squalor between Jericho's embattlements. This opulence was reflected particularly in the heavy festal celestial garb of the Babylonian moon god donned by the king as he assumed incarnation during the Spring Festival.

Transfigured as Sin, Keret paraded to the chants of ritual songs and lusty cries from the crowded square. *"To the places of the gods he goes on foot, the king shall go on foot. Seven times to all of them!"* Below the veranda the throng pulsed to violent pitch as the god—king proceeded down the steps to the sacral house of cultic worship and performed the sacred rites invoking fertility from the land over which he ruled. When he emerged in sunlight, a great cry of acclaim pronounced the god—king enthroned in proxy for another year. Absolution through the divine—king was renewed. The celestial liege of Jericho secured the city and ensured the crop for another growing season.

Jericho's unmatched, fourfold combination of wall, tower, well and army made it the most formidable citadel in the land. Its great storehouses of grain, replenished each harvest, could feed its residents for months on end. If Keret's soldiers failed to drive off an invading army, they could retreat behind the walls and the invaders would eat themselves out of provisions before the city would ever fall to siege.

The well was the invention of Keret's father, who once himself had raised an army of his tribesmen against the city of Jericho. Capturing the city, he had, under the threat of death, parlayed ransom of Jericho's former king in exchange for the bema now occupied by his son. Keret's father publicly executed the deposed king anyway. The new king added a second wall to the city for security. This outer retaining wall was fifteen feet high and constructed of large stones. Thirty feet inside this wall loomed the original barricade at the top of a sharp, angling, muddy slope. Sixteen feet thick, the top of this inner wall was wide enough for Keret's horsemen to race iron chariots two abreast with maneuvering room to spare. Altogether, the entire embankment provided nearly seventy feet of tactical defense.

Around this double ring of defense the sun-bleached skulls of those who had tried and failed to possess the Moon City oasis stared out through empty eye sockets as a warning to any would-be invaders. Such reminders of the violent, uncertain times and the inevitability of death were everywhere, not the least of which were the decorated skulls of their ancestors which the city's residents venerated and used to adorn the interiors of their houses. Strategically located at the bottom of Jordan's fertile valley and considered impregnable, Jericho gained a reputation as "the latch of Canaan."

There, built upon the outer wall as if its location depicted her calling, stooped Rahab's *khan*, her father's house. Rahab (which means "enlarge") had been given her name in days when her family's lack of everything had compelled Izun, her father, to offer his daughter to Sin, the supreme god of the ancient wilderness. The moon god was vengeful, lust-empowered and as dark in his mood as the black stones surrounding the city bearing his name. Kerech (as Sin was also called) was believed to possess the wilderness as his own and gave it to those who most emulated his despot ways. Standing stones in the houses, erected in the fields and bordering the road leading to the gate from the ford at Jordan all testified of Sin's ominous power over life and death. Sin controlled the seasons and the harvest as well as human fertility and destiny. And Jericho, the Moon City, was Sin's throne.

The central living quarters of Rahab's *khan* was, at most, three lengths the height of a man across, with floors of stone and clay plaster. A single window in a small storeroom provided her only source of relief from the stifling, urine-drenched and brutish air always rising from the city within. Whenever Rahab was not otherwise occupied spinning and drying flax or entertaining travelers received within the city gates, her siren's song drifted out of the window, mingling with the guttural discussions and jests of the watchmen in the tower.

Indentured to the king of Jericho from his own father's debts, Izun and his family had been destined for eternal serfdom and merciless days of thankless labor, just like all the rest of Jericho's poor who lived in squalor, their makeshift dwellings squeezed between the walls, if lucky, or in the shadow of the outer wall, if not. Only poverty awaited Izun and his family—until the day his youngest daughter was born, a child of extraordinary beauty that brought Izun his opportunity for deliverance.

Izun's first wife, mother of Rahab's nine stepsiblings, had died from a wasting disease. In spite of her family's many prayers and petitions, grain offerings and oaths over many days, she had passed into the netherworld. They had brought her bones with them when they had secured a house within the city at last. In keeping with custom, her painted skull, with seashells in its eye sockets, adorned the living quarters, keeping an eerie vigil, a reminder to all of the end of every man. The rest of her remains had been buried under the floor beneath their feet.

After the customary mourning period, Izun secured Asteroh as his second wife, but she had given him no sons. When the midwife announced the birth of a girl, Izun spat in disappointment into the running stream of waste that drained perpetually downward into the garbage heap of the tel. As he came into the stifling house, which was little more than a lean—to of goats' hair tarpaulin and poplar rods pitched in a spot of ground as close to the shadow of the outer wall as he could scrap from the other squatters, Izun glanced once at the swaddled babe and swore an oath.

"Rahab!" he barked, as if issuing an order to the babe. He turned his frowning scowl heavenward, his field-stained hands gnarled in hungry fists. "Keret! What need has a man of another girl? May my seasons change and cause you to enlarge my dwelling and cause the earth to bring forth favor and a name for my house!"

Asteroh, Rahab's mother, drew her veil across her mouth and followed her husband's oath with a hopeful prayer of her own, whispering "Aman" before she girded herself and rose to return to the fields where she bundled flax into heavy sheaves. In hope that his god would grant his desire, Izun had held the tiny new-born girl aloft as an offering in return for relief in days to come.

Little value was placed upon girl infants, particularly those born in poverty. The pinnacle of value that a woman might claim was the bride price offered as her dowry from a future husband or the favor and influence she provided in hospitality. But there would be no dowry for Rahab. Female fertility was thought to give power for the land's harvests. She would procure more as an offering to Sin. Canaanite tradition prized hospitality and all it provided above all else. The obligations of extending and receiving Canaanite hospitality were inviolate tribal traditions accepted and revered by all. Such hospitality included filling any request the guest might make. In exchange, a treaty of peace was established between the sovereign of the city-state and the guests who had accepted hospitality within its walls. This treaty carried mutual obligations of protection and alliance in wartime. Thus, once they accepted his welcome, any visitors, even potential enemies who had come to spy out the city and its defenses, were obligated to make peace with its sovereign.

Keret kept his own stable of personal courtesans, but beyond that, according to the traditions, he also extended the hospitality of his city-state to travelers and would-be invaders by welcoming them into the city's inns. It was at the tender age of 12 that young Rahab caught Keret's thirsty eye on the morning Izun fulfilled his vow. Following the flax harvest in the year she reached marriageable age, Rahab's father offered her to the king (and to Sin, the moon god) in accordance with the vow he had made at the Spring festival. In this way Rahab was bartered away by her father. She entered Jericho's *outer defense*, becoming part of Keret's unofficial hostelry, where she was made useful in the few ways that women were thought to be. In exchange for dedicating his daughter to the city, its king and its god, Izun was allowed to move his family into a house that was located on the outer wall.

From the beginning Rahab had shown a keen intuition and a disarming, winsome way with guests, proffering the liege of Jericho helpful and strategic intelligence. Although a caged bird, there was nothing frail about this beautiful young woman who served her conscription without complaint. She shrewdly used every guest and each morsel of news they divulged as leverage for climbing her way into the king's confidence, all the while aware that her success meant her family's security. Originally serfs and owners of nothing beyond their own determination to survive, Rahab and her family had risen from backbreaking stone—removal and service in Keret's outward corn and flax fields to becoming city dwellers. Indeed, it seemed Sin, the god of the moon had answered Izun's prayer.

In the years since Sin received Izun's and Asteroh's only child, Rahab's family had ascended to manage a small house of weavers, the most talented of which was Rahab's mother herself. Izun's daughter had brought him the protection and promotion he craved. And she continued to do so. His house was enlarged and he had gained favor in Jericho.

Izun was not unique. Rahab, and others like her, both men and women, young and poor, were living currency. They served as a hinge in the quest for security. Their lives secured the destiny of their impoverished family. Their service bought the allegiance of the king's enemies. In exchange for housing, food, business among the market merchants by day and trade in the king's other "treasury" by night, caravans came under Keret's protection and, therefore, under his control. Jericho remained the secure domain of its sovereign.

Salmon, a tribal prince of Judah, had been hand picked together with Yehoshaba to spy out this stronghold's defenses. These lions of YHWH were pure stock, descendents of the men who had brought Moses a good report of the land of Israel's promise. The nephew of one of Israel's mighty ones, Salmon was raised on the narrative of Caleb's mission when Moses led them to the brink of Promise.

In those days the flashing pillar of God's fire had hovered above the tabernacle just beyond the door of his family's tents. That generation's sudden deliverance from Egypt was as fresh in their memories as the cries of Pharaoh's drowning army when the great walls of the Red Sea came crashing down upon them. Recalling their amazement and awe at finding themselves dry-shod and safe on the far shore caused Miriam's outburst of praise to rise in their throats anew. Salmon and the other children would sit cross-legged, breathless, as old Caleb retold the hair-raising adventure of his first foray into Israel's promised land. Now, at last, Salmon and his people were returning to possess the territory promised to Abraham's descendants forever. The h'ivri[2] of this new generation followed in the dusty prints Joshua and Caleb had left on the dunes—a path long since erased by the forty years of desert winds during Israel's wilderness wandering.

*"They shall take no wife from the Canaanites for themselves."* These words of the fathers were inscribed on Salmon's heart as if the finger of God had put them there. The young h'ivri[3] warrior had never contended with YHWH's commands. Never, that is, until he and Yehoshaba had entered this house two days before. Now Salmon's heart wrestled with his conscience. It was unconscionable to compromise Israel's favor with YHWH now. Israel was a holy people, a unique treasure belonging to the Lord. For four decades, until the last of the former generation who had entered the wilderness died, this truth had been impressed upon Salmon and his brethren. They were called out, separated from the pagan nations all around. It was *tamei*, sin, to mix with the people of the land. How would Salmon explain to his uncle that their mission of secrecy had netted more than just details of the City of Palms' military strength?

Fire from within licked Salmon's neck and face as their hostess made her vow. It was hard to believe such a woman as this dwelt within the pagan stronghold. She was a woman with a different spirit, different even from the cowed or dull nature of so many of the women of his own tribe. Her every act attested to the sincerity of her heart and the breadth of her ability to believe in good to come.

The most telling, perhaps, was earlier this night when she had withstood the king's men at the door, feigning modesty and protesting their entrance to the inn while giving Salmon and Yehoshaba time to escape to the roof. The two men had heard the sounds of abuse below as they lay under the flax, arranged in heaps to dry in preparation for stripping and spinning into linen thread. She had refused to give them up even in the face of physical danger and had in fact sent the vanguard chasing into the wilderness in search of them.

"Quick now, Salmon!" Yehoshaba urged, tugging the sleeve of Salmon's cloak. Salmon's companion leaned nervously against the cold stones. "We must be going. The moon rises and our cover of darkness is fleeting!" Yehoshaba's urgent whisper was scarcely heard over the cadence of Salmon's surrendering heart.

Cautious was not a word that belonged to Rahab. From the first plateful of food she set before them, Salmon knew there was something different about her. Fair indeed, and wise with her words, a trait he expected Rahab had learned to use to her advantage in dealing with strangers as well as with street merchants. Though the "travelers" only accepted the comforts allowed by their God's commands, Rahab had laid siege to the fortress of Salmon's heart. In the hours he had spent gathering knowledge of the layout of the city and the strength and composition of the king's army, the prince of Judah had seen that Rahab's disarming outward charm was overshadowed by an even greater inner strength and decency.

"The people of this city have heard of your God. Their hearts melt with fear. The city's watchmen weave their own myths. Some say they have seen Him, sword in hand, standing on the plain during the night watch, keeping guard over your camp. I want to know this God of the Hebrews who shakes the wilderness and delivers His own from death."

Without husband or child, Rahab had a heart befitting a mother in Israel. Her countenance, brighter than the moonbeams falling out of the desert night, held Salmon's rapt attention. As he prepared to depart the city and return to Israel's encampment, Salmon knew this woman of unusual grace and courage had breached the walls of his heart and already ransacked the fortress of his will. She had persuaded him, but not by means of the flesh.

The night sky brightened. At the moment it seemed the celestial orb itself, worshipped by the king and residents of this formidable city-state, was determined to betray the spies to the king's watch as it rose. A short distance away, around the double circle of fortress walls, Jericho's tower revealed a single torchlight. Its flame of fire wavered intermittently as the scented desert breathed upon the signal post. An earlier foray had confirmed that there were always at least two men at arms keeping vigilance there by the hour.

"Our lives for yours," Salmon told the woman. "This is my oath."

"But news of our visit can be known to no one," Yehoshaba warned impatiently, his form partially in shadow just beyond a brightening shaft of silver light glancing through the single window cut in the wall of the house. That same wall served as the outer embankment of the stronghold the Hebrews had come to reconnoiter. "Else we are released from this vow."

The young spy's suspicion that Rahab would betray them to the king of Jericho was apparent. She could feel Yehoshaba's dark eyes icy gaze bore through her as he added in a harsh whisper, "I myself will extract the recompense from your father and brothers when God gives your city into our hand. If you betray us, not one of them shall live." Rahab's eye caught the slight movement of the Hebrew warrior's cloak as he grasped the hilt of his short sword, and she knew his words were in dead earnest.

It was not the Hebrew's sword that Rahab reverenced, however; it was his God. News of the victories of this army of former slaves over Sihon and Og, kings on the other side of the Jordan, had long since been the subject of nervous gossip in the side streets of Jericho's marketplace. Out of ear-shot of the king's guard, people both believed in and feared the Invisible God who allowed no image of Himself to be made. Was He spirit or did He take man's form as did the gods the Canaanites served? Rahab knew that even within his own house, Keret's subjects dreaded the children of Abraham whose cloud rose out of the south like a dark swarm of locusts on the horizon. This ominous force now lay encamped just across the river, plainly visible from Jericho's tower. For weeks, ever since harvest began, the whole city had been laying up grain against the siege they knew was coming.

"All whom you wish to save must be within these walls when we return," Salmon urged her for the last time. "The rest of the city will be given to the spear and torch."

Rahab let Salmon go. She hastened to the corner of the small storeroom where pottery jars filled with grain, evidence of recent siege preparations, sat in stacked pyramids among the bolts of thread she had spun for her father's weavers. Before either of the men could help her, Rahab had unfurled one of the spools of crimson twine she wound by day. Her fingers were tinged red from long hours of spinning and braiding the strands into bundles for the caravan baggage.

This fine crimson thread, used in the royal robes and festal garb of the king, along with the coveted bleached thread which was woven into the fine white linen so famous among the Egyptians, were the backbone of the local trade economy. Thread for the linen weavers and the hospitality of the *khan*— two measures of usefulness this young woman of Jericho had mastered.

Rahab stood upright, her arms filled with the loops of the great cord as though it were the lifeline of her existence. A flame of hope kindled in her heart as the two men recounted the stories of their God and their mighty deliverance from slavery. On the night of His visitation He had spared even certain Egyptians who fled to the refuge of Hebrew houses marked in the lamb's crimson blood.

"I know the Lord your God has given you the land," Rahab said. "Surely He shall give over this city as He did the cities of Sihon and Og. We have heard how the Lord your God parted the Red Sea so you could cross. The whole land faints because of you for His sake."

Rushing to the window as she spoke, Rahab bound the end of the scarlet thread to the twining hook in the wall. "Get into the mountain across from the city and hide there. After three days the king's men will give up their chase." She pushed the full length of bundled cord out the window, watching as it unfurled into the shadows until it reached within a man's height of the ground below. Then the keeper of the *khan* turned. "Please swear to me that when you come again you will remember my father's house to save it from destruction. What shall be the sign to me?"

Yehoshaba stepped to the window first. Grabbing the rope where it crossed the opening, he prepared to let himself down the wall, and said, "This cord of scarlet shall be bound in the window until we return. Then we shall know you have kept our mission to yourself." Glancing at his co-conspirator he finished, "Unless you bind this scarlet cord in the window through which you let us down, we shall be free from our oath and you and your house will perish." Tucking his outer garment into his belt, Yehoshaba exited the window, his weight pulling the cord taut.

Salmon leapt onto the sill after him. When the line went slack, Salmon wound it about his forearm as leverage for the descent. Without a further exchange of words between them, the prince of Judah and the harlot of Canaan bound themselves in their oath and he lunged away. When he came to the great, knotted end of the red cord and dropped to the desert floor, Salmon looked back. Rahab's face, pale and small against the black expanse of the wall of Jericho, still stared down at him. One crimson-stained hand upon the scarlet cord, the other clutched to her heart, Rahab watched in silence as Salmon turned and fled into the night.

Rahab stood by the window for a long time. The waters of the broad Jordan shimmered in the distance, dancing under the silvery gauze of the moon. Puffs of blue-white clouds drifted, carefree over the dome of the quiet sky. From the tower, the watch called out the curfew. Immediately after, there was a knock at the outer door. Following a brief and muffled exchange below, the maid who attended the inn's cooking fire stepped into the storeroom. "There are guests," she said quietly, and withdrew.

The voices of Izun and one of Rahab's step-brothers mingled with that of a stranger. "Rahab!" Izun's harsh voice called out as chairs scraped across the plastered floor. "Repast, girl! I have important guests!"

Obligation took over and, perhaps for the last time, Rahab prepared herself to entertain visitors to the *khan*. For the moment she put away the image of Salmon's face looking up at her from the foot of the wall. "Here I am, Father!" Rahab called back. "I'm coming just now."

Stepping away from her window and the world beyond, the harlot of Sin's city stronghold stopped at the small carved niche by the door and viewed her face in the golden light of a single oil lamp burning beside her bronze mirror. Lifting a pencil of *khol* she darkened the almond-shaped lines drawn around each eye. Rahab watched her own hand in the reflection as she smoothed the perfumer's balm across her neck. Her anklets chinked as she stepped into the khan's interior, the musky scent of her perfume trailing in the air.

Three days had passed and another seven. Salmon and Yehoshaba hid themselves in the caves of the limestone mountain across from Jericho until certain their pursuers from the city had given up the search. When they returned to the camp beyond the fords of the Jordan, Joshua received the spies' report with gladness and offered praise to God at hearing that the city had fallen into confusion and dread because of the Israelites. And to Salmon's great relief, the commander of Israel easily agreed to his request for Rahab and her house to be spared in return for saving their lives. "YHWH keeps His covenant," Joshua said, "and you shall keep the oath you made in His name. The woman from the inn and her family shall be delivered according to her faith. If we find her waiting upon the wall as she has sworn, the cord of scarlet shall be the sign."

Salmon closed his eyes and remembered the touch of Rahab's hand in those moments before his narrow escape from the king's men. He envisioned her fingertips stained crimson from dying and spinning the flax thread. Finally, his thoughts rested on his last sight of her: the vision of her rapt face looking down at him from the window as he fled the city.

Surely there would be trouble for her, Salmon thought, his brow furrowed with concern. He whinced as he remembered the rough soldiers blows he heard through the ceiling on the night she hid them from the king's vanguard. An entire spool length of crimson cord hanging out the window against the black stones and sun-bleached skulls of conquered foes of Jericho undoubtedly would arouse questions from the watchmen, if not from Rahab's own father. Certainly she would think of something to avert their inquiry. Had she not crafted a ready answer to cover him and Yehoshoba? Salmon prayed for Rahab's safety. He hoped with all his heart that she was as true as she seemed: valiant and steadfast to her word. Most of all, he hoped that the cord of red still hung from the window as ensign to her oath, binding her to the vow she had made; binding her to him.

Less than half a day's march away, the heavy, woven, scarlet line still hung from the courtesan's window. Rahab curled it up after the first watch was past each night. Her heart filled with renewed hope every time she looked out and saw from the lights in their camp that the Hebrews had not moved. But every morning, as the first bejeweled fingers of dawn reached over the purple mountains beyond the river, Rahab let the scarlet thread down again. This ritual kept alive day by day the promise the spies had made to her: *"Unless you bind this line of scarlet in the window through which you let us down..."*

Rahab fingered the thick red strands and remembered the warmth of Salmon's hand upon hers in the single touch they had exchanged. The great bundled knot at its end made a soft thumping rhythm against the night wall: *teh-thump, teh-thump, teh-thump.* This scarlet cord was Rahab's anchor in the storm. Throughout the city utter havoc reigned as fear and anticipation of the Israelite attack gripped the city's inhabitants. But Rahab was anchored by hope in the promise she held inside.

The chaos in the streets was motivation enough for Izun's family to gather together under one roof, as they had been now for several days. There was little relief from the closeness of the quarters, especially as the danger in the streets made venturing out of their enclave riskier with every passing day. Yet Rahab stolidly kept the visit from Israel's spies to herself. There were questions: Izun first, angrily decrying her spoilage of the valuable linen thread; then the vanguard passing on the wall. But in the end, concentrated panic had averted the attention even of Keret's foot soldiers, and they came no more to her door as before.

By now, Jericho's streets, houses and *khans* were crammed to overflowing with thousands of residents, including refugees from the unwalled villages under Keret's rule. Like the city's stacked, mud-brick houses, they seemed to tread every one on the next. Panic coagulated over the gathering storm, filling the putrid air with noise at all hours. Thievery and murder added to the chaos as conscienceless men took advantage of the looming catastrophe.

Faint wisps of smoke from the first cook fires came to Rahab on the predawn breeze, carried along with the lilting song of the bulbul and the cooing Egyptian turtledoves nestled in the yellow bulbs deep in the hearts of the feathery palms. A bright blue Indian kingfisher flitted amongst the scented balsams rising out of the earth at the edge of the cleared land adjoining the wall below her khan. What a contrast: the peaceful providence of joyful winged creatures going about their business, unthreatened and unfettered like every other day, against the noise and chaos of the human despair in the city. Rahab considered the irony. What must it feel like, she wondered, to be able to take wing at will and be carried on invisible wind currents high above the ground, able to fly away into another land entirely if so desired?

The variegated colors of the adjacent limestone mountain shifted in the first rays of light. The shadows of the caves dotting the face of its slopes were like so many open mouths whispering. One of them had hidden the escaping men just as she had upon her rooftop. One of them knew the secrets Rahab kept in her heart. Salmon had slept in one of those caves and there had prayed to his God. Had he prayed for her? She could not know for certain that he had indeed escaped, but the fact that the heads of Salmon and his companion had not been brought back on the spear points of the pursuing vanguard gave her great cause for hope. Those soldiers had returned to the city empty handed.

Suddenly, a small, brilliant tapestry of the richest color pallette caught Rahab's eye. Resplendent red, orange, and yellow feathers at each wing and an iridescent helmet of blue and green blending into its purple breast, a sun bird stopped in the cleft of a rock just beyond her window. Her breath, making a mist in the cool morning air, stopped. She looked for small signs every morning. Here was a sunbird far from its mate and nest. Perched on its high post, its head cocked slightly, the tiny aviator sang as if to her. Its introductory notes, like a greeting, were followed by a sweet sibilant warble which came to a crescendo on a low rapid musical trill. An unexpected tear stung Rahab's eye. The song seemed to hold the Voice of the Creator. In it she thought she heard hope. She found herself humming back.

Just then Rahab's tiny niece stumbled up from the pallet where they slept against the storeroom wall. Rubbing sleep and matted hair from her eyes, the child whimpered and came to cling to her aunt's knees. Rahab lifted her up, warm dampness from the thick night swaddle rested on Rahab's forearm as she cradled the little girl. The child shivered, as much from uncertainty over the rough human sounds already beginning without as from the ebbing chill of night. Rahab pulled the child inside her shawl as she stood by the window in the wall.

Bright specks of the torches of the fourth watch flickered out in the distance, disappearing one by one, extinguished by the morning sentries as they relieved the watchmen in the Israelite camp. Each one gave way to a fresh spark of anticipation and hope. *Perhaps this is the day for which I've waited.* The distant movement connected Rahab to a people not her own, strangers in a foreign land and rekindled the fire bed of her faith morning by morning. They would come. He would come for her. He had sworn.

Rahab's niece whimpered. Looking into the small fearful eyes, Rahab smiled. "Shhh. Don't be afraid." The songbird trilled again and then flew away. "La-la-la-la-li," Rahab began to sing as she cradled the girl in her arms. The words, fitted to the rhythm of her spindle in the days since the h'ivri had come and gone, were her own, inspired from the eyewitness accounts the spies gave her of their own deliverance from Egypt as children:

*"Shod and clothed, staff in hand,*
*get thee up out of this land.*

*Upon thy house deliverance red,*
*passing over Angel dread.*

*Mother, father, sister, kin,*
*no more slaves of master sin.*

*The River floods its banks and stands*
*while Israel crosses on dry sand!*

*Before their ark their God has gone.*
*Before His Angel goes the dawn!*

*Look He comes! Prepare the way.*
*Night has fled—here comes the Day!"*

## Endnotes

1. Joshua 6:15-17.

2. *H'ivri* was the term the Canaanites used for people from beyond the Euphrates. Abraham is first called H'ivri, the Hebrew, in Genesis 14:13.

3. *Hivari* is a term in Canaanite literature referring to raiding desert peoples who entered the land from Egypt.

*Chapter Four*

# Claiming Our Inheritance

Those were perilous days in Canaan, not unlike the circumstances faced by many women in our world today. With no law protecting the value of human life and every city-state vying for its own survival against the ruthless wilds, the only certainty was uncertainty. Into those dark days of lawlessness and peril the girl Rahab came, a daughter of destiny. Little did she know the plans God had for her, plans for her good and not for calamity, to give her *a future and a hope.*[1]

There, between the two great unbreachable walls of the pagan stronghold of Jericho, Rahab had lived her entire life. Having never left home and brought up in a grossly pagan environment, the only society and religion she had ever known, what chance did Rahab have of finding the true God? Nevertheless, God found her and gave her a new start. Rahab was heir to a glorious destiny, one she would never have dreamed of until the day the two Israelite spies awakened in her breast a hunger and a hope: hunger for a better life than the one she was living and hope for a brighter future for herself and her family in the company of the people of the one true God.

As a "commodity," the subject and product of a godless culture that neither esteemed women beyond the lure of their bodies nor could survive without them as producers of heirs, Rahab's life was one of use and abuse. Of mistakes and compulsion. Of disappointment and betrayal. She was in the uncomfortable position of never being truly "at home" anywhere: neither within the accepted circle of respectable society of Jericho's citizens nor outside the city, where wilderness, waste, wild beasts, and human marauders awaited.

Caught thus between two worlds, Rahab, the eternal outsider, recognized in the arrival of the two Hebrew scouts an opportunity to change her life. An alternative to the inevitability and hopelessness of her existence suddenly opened up before her. We have to admire her courage and determination in reaching out to take it. What opened her eyes? Did she believe in fate? In destiny? Or was she simply deeply impressed at the news of a God who actually *did* things for His people? A God who acted with awesome power on their behalf, in contrast to the gods of her own people, who were only horrible, bloodthirsty deities to be dreaded and appeased?

Whatever awakened the dream in Rahab's heart, when the door of salvation opened she stepped through it readily, considering what she would leave behind as nothing compared to the glory of a new start and a new life with God. Rahab used a painful past to make way for a blessed future. Throughout the ages and even today, Rahab's cord of scarlet still hangs in the window, an ensign of hope and victory and a promise of beauty for ashes for every woman (and man) who will reach out in faith and claim her (his) inheritance.

## Grafted into God's Family

During Israel's siege of Jericho, Rahab's family huddled together in their *khan* like the families of the spies had done the night of the first Passover—the very night they were delivered from slavery in Egypt. Restless and uncertain, this Canaanite family had nothing to depend on except the persuasiveness of this woman and her faith in the promise of deliverance. The scarlet cord hanging in the window testified and bound them to the oath of promise the messengers of salvation had made. It was their banner of protection, just like the Israelites' great deliverance from Egypt when the blood of lambs brushed upon the doorways protected them from the death angel: blood daubed there with the stalks of flax and hyssop from which Rahab stripped the thread she spun.

This simple act of faith would save them all in the end. Rahab summoned the courage to leave all she had known behind, to compromise any security in the familiar for the chance to cast her lot with a God whose power and awesome works she knew thus far only from hearsay. So great was the power of the faith Rahab exercised in those few critical days of visitation that her family—the family of the harlot—was grafted into the family of the King of kings!

And the greatest miracle of all, even greater than the city walls falling before the Israelites, was the fact that although the natural foundation of her dwelling was on that wall that fell all around, Rahab's whole house was saved by the strength of her faith. Imagine the rumbling, screams of terror and devastation that surrounded this tiny enclave where Rahab kept her family safe within the arms of her faith in the Lord God, the God of the messengers who had come to her inn.

The story of Rahab is proof of the ardent affections of God for a woman to whom life had dealt a sorry hand. It is the story of the hidden power of one woman's faith to open the door to that love. Acts of faith changed her life, the lives of her family, the history of her city, her nation and, in fact, the future of the entire planet! Rahab's is a story of the hidden power of a seemingly obscure woman's faith in action. Hers is a memorial to the power of one woman's response to the good news of covenant with the

God of the Bible. It is an eternal witness to how simple deeds done by the activation of faith from the heart can bring one from death to life. Small actions, even a single decision, can be the key to unlock a destiny boundless in its unfolding.

Rahab's story is a testimony to the faithful nature of the God of the Bible and His readiness to bind Himself in covenant to all those who seek Him, in spite of their past history or present circumstance. Everything is made new when He makes Himself known. In this story we see the true character of covenant. Regardless of one's past, one's poor or rich heritage and without restriction or limitation, simple deeds of faith in the covenant offered by God yield great rewards. Rahab chose to take a risk. She held firm in the hope she had for transformation. Instead of excuses, instead of weakness, she used the almost certain possibility of rejection and suffering, abuse and fear, to take a stand for all that was good and true and right. Mounting difficulties and the chaos all around her didn't change her mind.

Hers was the kind of faith that James commended as the only *true* faith:

> *What does it profit, my brethren, if someone says he has faith but does not have works? Can faith save him? If a brother or sister is naked and destitute of daily food, and one of you says to them, "Depart in peace, be warmed and filled," but you do not give them the things which are needed for the body, what does it profit? Thus also faith by itself, if it does not have works, is dead. But someone will say, "You have faith, and I have works." Show me your faith without your works, and I will show you my faith by my works.... You see then that a man is justified by works, and not by faith only. Likewise, was not Rahab the harlot also justified by works when she received the messengers and sent them out another way? For as the body without the spirit is dead, so faith without works is dead also.*[2]

Faith is the starting place for going anywhere with God. Faith has the power to move mountains and tear down strongholds, even as the walls of Jericho fell to the shouts of faith from the Israelites. That same faith preserved Rahab and her family as the walls of their city collapsed around them.

We have a dear friend named Jo whose life came to just such a crisis as the harlot of Jericho faced. Jo was hemmed in not by walls of stone but by mental walls of sexual confusion, spiritual deception and disbelief—walls just as strong and just as formidable as any that ever ringed the city of Jericho. But like the walls of Jericho, the walls around Jo's life were toppled by the power of God released through faith. And, like Rahab of Jericho before her, Jo found a great deliverance.

## Free at Last!

When Jo attended the February 2000 "Daughters of the Lion Conference," she was in a committed alternate lifestyle. Raised in traditional Christianity, the adopted daughter of middle class Americans, she had been the victim of sexual abuse and suffered from an identity crisis that affected all the interior realms of her being. Ironically, Jo had been "liberated" and found her "identity" through associations she made at the Baptist Union youth events on her campus. Twelve years later, when Jo was fully engaged as an outspoken "poster girl" of the "in your face" homosexual community and was in a committed same—sex relationship of several years duration, her sister, whose life had been radically altered by a visitation from God, invited Jo to the conference. Here is what happened, in her own words:

As I drove into the warehouse complex, I knew something big was about to go down, but the only thing I could do to mask my hopeful excitement was mock the "signs and wonders" that I heard would be seen. Four of my friends squeezed into three chairs, and that was the first miracle, because no one complained that they were uncomfortable; there was far too much to look at and take in!

Finally, it began. The music, the tambourines, the shaking, the shouting...what in the world was happening? Although my parents sat silently behind me, I think they were in shock that I was at the conference. It had only been nearly 12 years that they had been praying for me to come to the Lord! As a matter of fact, my mom had discovered what she calls "the Chavda conferences," and had started a mini-watch at her house, where prayer for my salvation and deliverance greatly intensified.

Then one of my friends said, "Let's clap; we'll blend in better!" So we all methodically clapped to an unfamiliar rhythm. Looking around me and staring at every person—on the floor, in the middle of the aisle, shaking and crying—it sure wasn't like being in public where people can tell if you are staring at them. So I announced, "Look around and feel free to stare; they sure won't notice!" So we clapped, we stared and we began to relax. Seeing that we weren't ready to run out, my mom tapped me on the back and said, "Go dance in the aisle."

"You'll never catch me dancing in this church!" I snapped back.

Something began to change. The music slowed down. I literally felt like I was not in the same room. What was that sound? I didn't understand it. What were they saying? How did they all know the same song? It was another language. I wanted to hear more. Something was very different now. The woman on the platform announced that the "Angel of the Lord was here." "Where?" I thought. I didn't see anything. Where was He? Then everyone in the room gasped—a golden dust was in the air and caught in a Bible! The very thing I had mocked had happened before my eyes! Now I believed. But the most significant moment was about to happen.

Pastor Mahesh walked up to the front of the crowd, held up his hands, which were golden from the manifestation, and shouted, "Let the King of Glory...COME IN!" I suddenly felt anxious. I wanted to check my pockets for a ticket. I was convinced that Jesus was about to appear. "I almost missed it," I said to myself. "I almost missed it! I barely made it! Jesus is coming back...do I have whatever is required to go with Him when He arrives?" I was excited and fearful at the same time.

Then Pastor Mahesh said it again. "Let the King of Glory...COME IN!" Instantly I heard the sound, starting on my left and going around the back of me all the way to the right, of huge steel doors slamming shut one after the other. Then a voice said, "I have closed the doors of your past...and I am sealing them shut!" I felt as if I were standing in front of a new open door. It was at that precise moment that I finally took a deep breath and exhaled what I had been holding in for 12 years. I knew that I would no longer live the life of a lesbian. I literally no longer had that identity or desire. It was like someone took that heavy object out of my hand, and I no longer had to carry it. I stood there in shocked silence. It was too much to sort through in my mind. I had only been in that warehouse for a little more than an hour. Could this be real?

One of the speakers that night shared her testimony of how the Lord healed her and delivered her from a situation that had no hope. At one point, gripping her jacket, she expressed how the only real thing any of us had was Jesus, and if we didn't know what to do or where to turn, "Hold onto Jesus! Just hold on, He will not let you go." There was a moment while she was speaking when gold-like particles, as out of thin air, covered her from head to toe! I felt that to "hold on" was all I could do!

I demanded that my friends get in the prayer line with me, and we ended up waiting for 45 minutes! People were falling all over the room. I felt anesthetized. We walked in a straight line, like kindergartners, holding hands as if to protect one another by doing whatever was about to happen together. We put our toes on the line of gray duct tape on the floor at the front of that room of more than a thousand people. Myself, a lesbian for 12 years, my friend, who had just entered the gay lifestyle, a co-worker who was 5 months pregnant out of wedlock and my boss, who was raised Pentecostal; there we were, all holding hands together!

My gay friend and I looked at one another and vowed, "We are not going down!" But I wanted to see that gold stuff up close. Suddenly, my eyes started getting a milky glaze over them, and I could hardly see anything! Something like a wave of electricity went through me, and one of my friends collapsed on the floor. The woman ministering simply laughed kindly as she stood in front of me. Then she kissed me on the cheek. In an instant, I too was falling down in a blanket of the Presence of God that was more real and wonderful to me than my girlfriend waiting for me at home or anything in that church. Twenty minutes later we all opened our eyes, lying side by side in stunned silence. My parents were silently watching from a distance.

I managed to get to my car and, once alone, the tears came. "Lord," I said, "I am so sorry, but for so much that I don't know where to start." A perfect peace washed over me. As I drove home in that Presence, the oil that had been touched to my forehead during the prayer was multiplying and oozing all over me. At the same time it was as if a holy salve had anointed the eyes of my heart, and scales from many things were falling off. I knew there was an open door in front of me. That door was Jesus and His moment of destiny in my life.

The next night, I raised my hand in what I thought was a survey by Pastor Mahesh of those who didn't speak in tongues. I joined a group of more than 20 people and began to speak in tongues. It felt so natural. Again, that anesthetized feeling came over me as I moved to the prayer line. Mahesh prayed for me, and I was out like a light. It was as though my life were a child's flip book passing before my fluttering eyes as deliverance from the hurt and devastation of all those things I had willingly and unwillingly experienced took place. When it was over, I felt like Cinderella at the ball in the fairy tale. There was light all around me, and in that light my desires were transformed. Thirty minutes later I heard my mom's voice as they had been searching for me in the mass of people. I literally bumped into my father as I managed to stand. I was instantly reconciled with my family after twelve years of distance and conflict. My parents were in shock. The next day my mom told me that seven years earlier Bonnie had given her a word: "The Lord has heard your prayers for your children, and your daughter will return to her borders."

In the time since that conference God has brought me into employment for a well-known Christian ministry and has entrusted me with a position of leadership in my local church. I can't imagine where I would be today if my sister, my mother, and my father had not been relentless to pray and believe in the power of the Lord's hand. Today, I know who I am. I am a daughter of the Lion of the tribe of Judah. I am part of a family, both natural and spiritual, that is irreplaceable. I live in a nation that affords us the freedom to worship Jesus freely and embrace all He has. I found my ticket; it was repentance, it was forgiveness, it was love, it was family, it was the Holy Spirit, it was Jesus, it was choosing to be a part of my natural family and my spiritual family.

Free at last, free at last, thank God almighty I am FREE...AT...LAST!"

## Escape into Grace

As Jo's testimony illustrates, Rahab represents any modern day woman whose *kairos* moment suddenly rises out of the dust and storm of disappointment, danger and chaos that life presents. Jo thought she knew herself. She thought she had found her identity as a woman in a life of lesbianism. Twelve years of deception and growing disillusionment followed before she found her *true* identity: *a daughter of the Lion of the tribe of Judah.* It is only in union with Christ that we discover who we really are and who we are meant to be.

This is the message of Rahab, an exchange of faith between God and man. Rahab's story is a testimony to the humility and sincerity of the Father of the Lord Jesus Christ. Salvation and restoration of individual hearts is His ultimate prize. He desires every person, in every generation, from every nation and culture to escape into His saving grace. From the oldest city in the world, out of the oldest profession known to man, comes the oldest story in history—the story of redemption. The faith of one woman against whom all the odds of life had stacked themselves was woven into the tie that binds. A harlot dedicated to Sin, the moon-god, became the daughter of deliverance for her family, transferrring her and her lineage into the family of the King of kings!

*The book of the genealogy of Jesus Christ, the Son of David, the Son of Abraham:*

*Abraham begot Isaac, Isaac begot Jacob, and Jacob begot Judah and his brothers. Judah begot Perez and Zerah by Tamar, Perez begot Hezron, and Hezron begot Ram. Ram begot Amminadab, Amminadab begot Nahshon, and Nahshon begot Salmon. Salmon begot Boaz by Rahab, Boaz begot Obed by Ruth, Obed begot Jesse, and Jesse begot David the king.*[3]

From victim to victor, Rahab's name was taken off the cursing lips of immoral men and placed by the Savior Himself upon the prayers and veneration of the righteous. Once doomed to disappear in obscurity, lost forever in the shifting sands of ancient Canaan, Rahab's legacy lives on even today. The record of her singular act of faith has been preserved in the very Word of God itself, encouraging and enlightening all who will take the time to learn its lesson.

And that lesson? *Faith in the one true living God will change your destiny forever.* No matter what crisis you face, no matter where you have been or what you have done, if you turn in faith to God and cast yourself on His mercy you can escape into His marvelous grace, forever free from your sin and the consequences of your past. You can claim the inheritance God has prepared for you since before the foundation of the world. It means recognizing and seizing your *kairos* moment—your moment of destiny—when it comes. As Paul, quoting Isaiah, appealed to the Corinthians:

> *We then, as workers together with Him also plead with you not to receive the grace of God in vain. For He says: "In an acceptable time I have heard you, and in the day of salvation I have helped you." Behold, now is the accepted time; behold, now is the day of salvation.*[4]

"Now *is* the day of salvation."

Rahab recognized that day when it came her way. Her circumstances propelled her into the *kairos* moment of her spiritual destiny prepared beforehand by God. Her simple acts of faith, converging over a few days of her life, have forever inscribed her in the world's best selling book as one of its premier heroines. Simple acts of faith such as hers can change history, create the unimaginable and make the impossible possible:

> *Now faith is the substance of things hoped for, the evidence of things not seen. For by it the elders obtained a good testimony...By faith the walls of Jericho fell down after they were encircled for seven days. By faith the harlot Rahab did not perish with those who did not believe, when she had received the spies with peace.*[5]

In light of Rahab's miraculous testimony, the writer of Hebrews tells us that God's plan for us in the new covenant encompasses more than just the redemptive restoration of our own circumstances. It can touch all those within our circle of influence. Because Rahab trusted God and acted on her faith, her entire household was saved from destruction.

Right now, from today, let your faith fly uncaged and fully activated. Don't just believe for yourself, but believe that the covenant God has with you also extends to those you love and hold as your family members. You can become a lightning rod of deliverance from evil on their behalf.

## Sexual Confusion

Through faith, Rahab stepped into her true identity, the lineage of the King. Her story speaks to the importance of identity and impact of a woman's sexuality upon herself, her family, her community and her people. Traditionally, and almost universally, a woman's worth has been connected to her outward appearance, her physical beauty and her reproductive prowess. How do we address these issues; issues related to a body that is temporal and which have generational and possibly eternal impact on society?

One of the greatest travesties of contemporary Western Christianity was its failure to respond effectively and spiritually to the cultural revolution of the 1960s. Despite the outpourings of the Latter Rain movement in the '40s; the rise of evangelists such as Oral Roberts and Billy Graham in the '40s, '50s and '60s; and the Jesus and Charismatic movements of the '70s and '80s, the Church failed to address the cultural issues that were causing a sea of change in Western society. The consequences of this failure for women and their seed after them are inestimable.

Because Judeo-Christian theology had never answered the hard questions about women, the sexual revolt that began on college campuses in America went global. At its core were issues of equality and freedom of choice. Both were cries for liberation in response to the age-old double standard that has prevailed in nearly every area of society. In both church and secular society, women have often been relegated to the status of children; they are expected to be "seen and not heard"! But determinedly, God is keeping His word to Eve. And just as Jeremiah promised, *"For the Lord has created a new thing in the earth—a woman shall encompass a man."*[6]

Like the outer walls of Jericho in Rahab's day, the importance and influence of women are key to the viability and success of any family, church, business or any other institution. And, as with Rahab, a woman's opportunity comes with responsibility. That word itself begins with "response," the essential element of faith.

## Endnotes

1. Jeremiah 29:11.
2. James 2:14-18, 24-26.
3. Matthew 1:1-6.
4. 2 Corinthians 6:1-2.
5. Hebrews 11:1-2, 30-31.
6. Jeremiah 31:22b.

# Chapter Five

# Daughter of the King— or Daughter of Bondage?

A woman's sexual identity is as important to her life journey as the compass a traveler takes into the wilderness. Like that compass, a woman's sexual identity must point to true north if she is to find her way "there and back again." If her compass is not true, the farther she goes on the journey, the farther off course will she stray from her intended destination.

"True" does not necessarily mean being true to oneself but rather true to something or someone more sure than one's individual perspective and personal experience. A woman's sexual history need not construct her sexual identity. Ideally, a woman should derive her identity from the God who made her, and that identity should affect everything else in her life, including her sexuality.

Jo, whose story you read in the last chapter, is a good example. Raised in the church, Jo nevertheless became confused in her personal and sexual identity as a woman. She thought she found it in women's liberation, feminism and lesbianism, but discovered that those were all lies. Only in Christ did she find her true self and true liberty.

Only in Christ did she find the release to be the daughter of the King and the woman she was created to be.

## Rejecting Eden

Modern feminism, in most cases, loves to dismiss Eden as an absurd old wives' tale or the sadistic epic of a male chauvinist Patriarch calling himself God. Yet the drama of Eden almost laughably remains the ulterior obsession of nearly every feminist theoretician.

There are a couple of simple fallacies in postmodern feminism that are the result of rejecting Eden. First, the feminist movement is living on the borrowed pain of women's lives other than their own, including Eve's! This is especially true in the West. The second fallacy is the absurdity of a woman assuming that, being the creation, she knows more about herself than does the One who created her.

After the fall, creation was subjected in hope: hope in the certainty of redemption promised when God subjected it. If we listen, we can hear it groaning all around us: "This is not what we will be." In rejecting our roots, Feminism has lost its way on the journey toward redemption. One may not like the parents they are born of, but they remain nevertheless one's parents. So it is with Adam and Eve. Eden has something to teach us, and we must be careful to learn.

Women, in particular, are searching for significance in our generation. There is a holy restlessness concerning purpose as much as the yearning for power. Deep calls unto deep.

Modern neo-pagan cults have joined with the postmodern women's movement to reject the events of creation in the Bible as being anti-woman. But, seeing the plan of God come almost full circle in our own day, it appears much more likely that the sin our first parents took out of Eden has more to do with the status of women through the ages than any ill will of God.

The serpent, that "old man of sin" who deceived Eve and overcame Cain, is still trying to get the upper hand and make human misery ever worse. But we shall rule over him because of the promise God made to Eve: "Your seed shall crush his head." History waited upon two great events affecting the destiny of the woman God had made: Calvary and Pentecost. In the first, the second Adam accepted the deep sleep, and out of Him has come the woman God is building into a helper fit for Him. And this time, believe it, she-is-it! In the second event, woman's glory was restored. She received back her voice as the Rushing Spirit of God was poured out in His name to be with and within young and old, male and female.

On this side of Eden, women have perhaps suffered the most concerning the loss of their original destiny. Even more tragic is the fact that in this day the God-given heritage of modern-day women has been stolen by secular forces that claim to be discovering it.

## The Ultimate Woman

"Like a bear robbed of her cubs" is an old euphemism alluding to the fact that there is no more lethal danger than a woman whose seed has been stolen. Yet modern feminism has done exactly that. It has stolen the heritage of every woman it seduces. In the name of liberation the very nature of womanhood is under attack in the evolution of the godless so-called women's movement. But a counterfeit is only as good as its semblance to the real thing! Modern feminism offers the wrong answers to the right questions. Those questions are as old as the fall, and in order to offer true solutions to them we must start in the beginning with the very first woman made by God.

The true female identity of every woman was formed in the image of God. Eve, as originally built by God from Adam's rib, models every woman's right and heritage. The ultimate woman is the counterpart of man. She is neither independent nor co-dependent, as the secular feminists claim, but interdependent as one brought forth to complete the mission of humanity. The ultimate woman is able to lead as well as follow. She is a life giver and mother, defender of the innocent, naïve, and young.

The modern feminist rant focuses on what has been called the "kernel" of patriarchy: Somebody has to be in charge and that somebody has to be male. They consider the suppression of the female gender to be the root problem of all race and inequality issues worldwide. This is where they make the hyper-leap back to the Garden of Eden and assume that God, the great Patriarch in the sky, set things up this way.

But did He? A daughter has no greater ally or fiercer champion than a father who believes in her. Does it make any sense that the Captain of Hosts, in death lock against the forces of evil and willing to die for the object of His affection, would begin by immobilizing more than one half of His fighting force simply because they wear bras? If we suppose for a moment that we have viewed "Garden events" through dim and darkened eyes, as the Sioux holy man suggested, then we have been reading the vision all wrong.

When God said to Eve, "He shall rule over you," was He putting Eve under Adam's feet or was He simply letting her know what was coming? In the same breath God said that Eve's seed would put the serpent's offspring to heel. A few scenes later sin appears as a character waiting to pounce on Cain, and God warns Cain not to let sin get the upper hand. It appears then that sin, not men, has stolen the ruler's scepter.

There is a simple solution for those humble enough to hear. As with everything God does, the answer lies not in a theorem or a dictum but in a Person. His solution is a feminist activist, the Seed of a woman, who ate the entire Tree of Death and came back to tell about it. Now this Seed, Jesus Christ, holds the ruler's scepter and extends it to whomever will receive it.

It is the unique province of women to protect, defend, build up and be the fruit—bearing catalyst in the garden of society, whether secular or religious. No man can bring a woman's distinctive contribution to the table, boardroom, sanctuary, or bedroom. In the Godhead the Holy Spirit is a type and role model for the ultimate woman. Equal to the Father and the Son, He is the "power" and very present influencer of all God does. God has written Himself into the history of humankind through the Person of the Holy Spirit. Often that history has been wrought through the vessel of a woman. His types in Scripture include figures who typify the hidden power of a woman. We have seen several examples of this already in previous chapters.

## The Fruit No Longer Resembles the Root

Modern day evangelicals and charismatics tend in many ways to reflect ancient pagans more than they do ancient Christians, at least the Christians of the first century. For the first hundred years or so after Pentecost the "new thing" that Joel and Jeremiah spoke of was at work in the church. But after all the original eyewitnesses had died off, traditions and theology developed that took the church in some wrong directions until, before long, the fruit no longer resembled the root! The biggest losers were the women.

In many pagan religions and modern neopagan cults, Eve is worshiped as the mother goddess. She might well deserve this title because she, in fact, could be called the first inventor of her own theology. One has only to ask most postmodern evangelicals or charismatics about their personal faith and practice to discover that their beliefs and attitudes resemble those of ancient pagans more so than of the first Christians and not because of their morality. Postmodern individualism in the Christian faith is mostly self-styled according to what someone perceives his or her own needs are in relation to God and, ultimately, what feels "good" or "right." For the most part, this "self-styled" religion is disconnected from any sound doctrine, or if it has sound doctrine, the morality of personal practice tends to be inconsistent with what one says he or she believes.

Post modernism has brought us full circle in this respect. In this age, the trend of Christians and pagans alike is designer religion according to one's individual opinion and invention. The old is considered irrelevant to the new and much of authentic theology is largely dismissed. The result is that, unlike the faith of early Christians whose theology and morality were two sides of one coin, Christians today rarely know what they believe anymore, especially in terms of theology. Even rarer are Christians who know *why* they believe what they do. Rarer still are those who live consistently according to what they profess to believe. In the old days of Christianity, in the first century A.D., defining what one believed was as important as what one did. A man acted according to what he understood in his belief.

How much of what we believe about women has been shaped by our drift from God's original design? Has God changed what He believes about women, or have we lost sight of His plan? When the serpent came to Eve in the garden, his deception was in offering her everything that she *already* possessed. Woman at her creation was perfect in form, power, dominion and nature. It was the use of her desire out of harmony with God's desire that corrupted creation. Lucifer was the seal of perfection, perfect in all his way *until iniquity was found in him.*[1] The Bible calls iniquity rebellion and lawlessness, literally meaning to go one's own way in opposition to the will of God. But One has come, humble and obedient even unto death. Iniquity and the curse has been broken. He is the Way back to Eden, to the spotless Bride.

Origin authenticates. For this reason the original of anything has a certain immutable authority. This is why, for instance, a person finds identity in knowing the way of his ancestors or hearing the stories of his grandparents. Concerning the theology of women, we have two clear scriptural examples outlining God's original intent. First we have the account from Eden. But what do God's words, few as they are concerning the woman in the original story, have to teach us, and what do we have to learn? "After dinner," when God, seemingly allowing for the fact she had been enticed, told Eve that two basic aspects of her life were about to change: "I will multiply, multiply your pain from your pregnancy with pains shall you bear children. Toward your husband will be your lust, yet he will rule over you," what did this mean to those born like her? Until then everything was pretty much "very good." Did this permanently demote woman to second class everything? What has it to do with sin? And what has it to say about a woman who has neither children nor husband? Second, we have the Book of Acts and the accounts of women's roles and leadership in the early church from the Epistles. What does Pentecost, the fulfillment of Joel 2 and the resulting rise of women in leadership of the early church have to tell us about God's redemptive plan and restoration of women by the work of the Cross?

Our human identity is found in the One who formed our first parents in the Garden. This necessitates that everyone of us receives the gospel of Jesus Christ, for only by finding our Brother, lost to us for so long, can we find the way home to Father again. Those who recognize the Anointed One only as a philosopher will always be asking questions of questions. Those who only know Him as a prophet will be looking for the One to come. But those He draws into the chamber and shows Himself as their Father's Son will find both food in famine and life from death.

Looking to the beginning, we see things in a clearer light. The advent of the Christian faith at Pentecost propelled women to the forefront of redemptive history. The "culture of life" within the early Christian counterculture rapidly produced a substantial surplus of females. For the first century or so, the entire world was an unreached people group as far as Christianity was concerned. We have already observed that the Christian faith, because of its truly liberating characteristics, proved to be very appealing to women. The high rate of conversion among women resulted inevitably in frequent marriages between Christian women and pagan men. Overall, the abundance of Christian women enjoying the benefits of the Christian "culture of life" resulted in higher birthrates, lower infanticide as more value placed on baby girls increased the number who were allowed to live and mature into women, and superior fertility. In other words, by sheer numbers alone, women contributed significantly to the rise of Christianity!

These same life and equality values were espoused by the early founders of the women's movement. Yet, modernity has hijacked those values, stealing the true destiny and heritage of women along with them. The secular argument for women's rights has moved from its origins on biblical equality and the end of "child murder" (as the originators called abortion) to a push for the right to abort at will and a sexual revolution promoting lesbianism. Both of these issues are counter productive to the future of women and women's health. Eve has been seduced once again!

## The Feminist Deception

Feminist consciousness is emerging as a spirit of the age and has become a global trend. In the beginning, no doubt, it was an individual trend, but it has now become a movement and even a school of thought popular among the writers of modern sensibility. In truth, woman was created to ultimately carry and bring forth life, as Eve's very name indicates. The immutable principle of "life in the seed" exists in every refraction of creation. From the moment of genesis the spiritual destiny of that seed is to triumph over the powers of spiritual repression that come to kill, steal and destroy woman and her children.

But we see also that woman alone, like man alone, is only half of the equation, be it relationally, socially, governmentally, economically or religiously. Radical feminist theory is deceptive and dangerous in that it promotes a world where woman alone is enough and, in fact, preferable. The redemptive struggle, begun by the Holy Spirit at the rise of the Western women's equality move, has been hijacked no less than the immediate design for Eve was interdicted by the serpent's subtle lies. Today we see the fruit of that robbery alive and well as the core element of the degradation and repression of the female.

Hope is alive and well, however, because there is another outpouring occurring today, an outpouring of promise, ancient and new, for women everywhere in every circumstance. It behooves every daughter alive to come to herself in full recognition of her true identity. Women bear a great responsibility in God's redemptive plan. The Holy Spirit hovers over all that is in chaos waiting to overshadow the woman as He did Elizabeth and Mary in the gospels and as He did Rahab in Jericho so long ago.

*The hidden power of the woman is in assuming the identity God has designed for her beforehand.* For many in this generation this means receiving the messengers of God's covenant. It requires revelation. It may involve confrontation. It certainly means deliverance from all that opposes God's intention. And it may mean a transformation as radical as Rahab's from khan keeper to matriarch of Judah! But after all, the daughter of a lion is also a lion. That means her spiritual genetic code carries the same structure as the Man who laid down his life on Calvary that the second Eve might be brought from His side to be fashioned into His Bride.

The satanic strategy begun in Eden was to formulate a plan to prevent Eve and her seed from giving or receiving life. Women's sexual identity is at the heart of this battle. Confusion over that identity continues to sideline and misdirect countless women today, even as they mistakenly believe they have found "liberation" and purpose in feminism. If women are to reach their true destination and make a path of life for their daughters to follow, they must undertake a journey that begins and ends in the destiny God has ordained for the gender as well as for each individual woman. Life to life, her seed is meant to show forth the glory of God. And He is not in an identity crisis!

## It Is Time to Return to Our Roots

In order to be legitimate and truly worthwhile, the feminist movement must return to its roots. The women who founded the movement in the 19th century were devout Bible believers with a threefold purpose of abolishing the enslavement of Blacks, granting women equal voice and power in government and ending abortion. All of these they saw as similar in that they elevated the value of human life. How appropriate, then, for the daughters of Eve to come to the defense of these core principles!

The feminist movement that so shaped the 20th century did not originate with Marxist socialism, secular humanism or even theological liberalism. It was the direct outgrowth of the great evangelical and holiness revivals that swept America and England in the 1800s. Hardly a last shallow gasp of that original spirit remains in the organized women's movement today, but its tirade grows louder and louder. The current move to remove Judeo-Christian faith from the public square rages like a brushfire on a dry grassy plain. Women are in the cross hairs, if not by oppression and repression, then by giving them a liberation leg up into making desire equal to destiny. As long as woman's desire is clothed in temporary mortal flesh it must be checked by God's desire for her!

The apostle Paul captures the whole of it in his letter to the Ephesians. He too is a prisoner, unjustly chained by the religious systems of his day, but he doesn't focus on the chains. Rather he stays focused on aligning himself to the purpose of God!

*I, therefore, the prisoner of the Lord, beseech you to walk worthy of the calling with which you were called...(There is) one God and Father of all, who is above all, and through all, and in you all. But to each one of us grace was given according to the measure of Christ's gift. Therefore He says: "When He ascended on high, He led captivity captive, and gave gifts to men...that He might fill all things...that we should no longer be children, tossed to and fro and carried about with every wind of doctrine, by the trickery of men, in the cunning craftiness of deceitful plotting...This I say, therefore, and testify in the Lord, that you should no longer walk as the rest of the Gentiles walk, in the futility of their mind, having their understanding darkened, being alienated from the life of God, because of the ignorance that is in them, because of the blindness of their heart; who, being past feeling, have given themselves over to lewdness, to work all uncleanness with greediness.*

*But you have not so learned Christ, if indeed you have heard Him and have been taught by Him, as the truth is in Jesus: that you put off, concerning your former conduct, the old man which grows corrupt according to the deceitful lusts, and be renewed in the spirit of your mind, and that you put on the new man which was created according to God, in true righteousness and holiness.*[2]

Indeed, all thinking that does not hold God and His worldview as its core will ultimately prove futile and fatal! When the truth of Christ is not the source of your identity, decision, conversation, and mission—when there is no "G" (God) factor—your conclusions will be vain, worthless, empty, and completely lacking intelligent understanding.

And yet that is exactly where mankind as a whole has been getting it wrong since Eden. Modern man's tendency to define God's attributes and invent his own religion according to his own desire is nothing new. When enticed, our mother took a swipe at it herself. In an exaggeration of God's instruction, Eve told the serpent, "If we even touch it we'll die!" Then she turned right around, contemplated the thing that she had just claimed would kill her, and decided to try it. Generally speaking, isn't this human nature? Ethos, logos, pathos; Eve ate what she found desirable in the moment. Even the beginning of human freewill showed an ability to use the ethics, logic and passion created by God to strive for something other than His desires.

Liberation is on the hearts and minds of oppressed societies throughout the world today, as typified by the many conflicts in the Middle East and other places. *The contemporary women's movement, such as it is, embodies the most serious threat to women by offering them the false identity of vain philosophies in the guise of liberty.*

The essential expression of the feminist movement today is found in *gynocriticism*, a term coined by Ellen Showalter to describe the writings of women (novels, poetry, drama, essays, letters and journals) edited by women. Gynocritical studies deal with female imagination, feminist language and the experience of women expressed in literature. Unfortunately, these "champions" of equality wrestle for the equal rights of all and of all views *except* the biblical view and the voices of persons who espouse it.

Gynocriticism embodies the subject matter of women's studies in most colleges and universities today. Almost invariably, the goal of instruction in women's studies programs is sexual identity crisis with the solution being found in female solstice, specifically lesbianism. But the strategy does not stop there. The diatribe of a great many of these so called sages and professors blends into a rage against the male gender. It has intensified to the point of violent exclusion of all males and their influence and the promotion of the ultimate Amazonian utopia by partnering genetic engineering and reproductive science methods!

Thus, our greatest treasures and our future inheritance are in grave danger. Like every other aspect of the revelation of God, His covenants and His purpose for humankind, women's sexual identity can be resolved only in the context of healthy hetero-social perspective.

When foreign armies overran Jerusalem, they took the children of Israel captive and made them carry the beloved holy furniture and treasures of the temple away to be abused in pagan rituals. Rabbinical tradition holds that the prophet Jeremiah saw mother Rachel come out of her grave in Bethlehem and stand by the road weeping as she watched her daughters go into bondage. "A voice was heard in Ramah, lamentation, weeping, and great mourning, Rachel weeping for her children, refusing to be comforted, because they are no more."[3]

The following piece, written by a Christian mother, expresses her perspective on this emerging global feminist influence. In it, a woman's prophetic specter keeps vigil for the future of her daughters as the philosophies that underlie feminist expression threaten feminine destiny and disdain womanhood itself. Titled "Lament," it speaks of the fruitlessness and despair lesbianism presents as the expression of women's sexuality.

## Lament

To write what first was dreamt in visions on eons of cruel time and preserved in ice floes while their pressure builds and threatens our only ship that here lies frozen, waiting, hoping for the thaw before its hull is fully crushed and with it our last chance of carrying them, our daughters, to escape: To you, mothers, I call! Before the broken ship sinks and falls beneath an unrelenting glacial surface sea. Champion awake! Defender rise! Lion and bear be loosed. Your daughter's daughters lie within this ship's belly, lambs in open country.

Wisdom stands at the head of every street. "To you, Eve's true daughters! To you I call!"

So shatter our dull prim silence that forbids us speak while pretender mothers seduce with serpent tongues our next of kin. Tongues on loan from ancient Garden, they flick them in and out and draw their inner poison to the fang. "Taste," the serpent in them whispers. The ancient Star of Morning smiles. "Has God really said?" he asks. "Taste!" false women shout. "Delightful to make one wise...delicious food." They coil and strike, sending twice-dead fruit devouring down into our virgins' veins. "Who doth forbid us bread of our own choosing?"

New Eve hear them not nor listen! Life-giver, tear down their sepulcher altars!

No mothers these: Beauvoir, Friedan, Alice B., Daly or Cixous, Lacan's prodigious spire. Sartre has done enough abusing! Deceitful sisters, lascivious brothers. Horse of Trojan these, Pandora's ireful sprite. No guides, they! No goddesses self-reborn. No lamp of revelation. No mirror of inner truth. This ill harmonious chorus sings and begs new voices to the band. Thief, robber, destroyer. Their screeching calls to vacant deep where user had his way and now they seek to draw true woman out to murder, giving her their voice instead of ours. Instead of mine.

Hail and fire rain down where Lot's wife cast her gaze behind her back to watch while molten brimstone sulfur seeks to find our daughters' flesh as meat.

Treacherous. Claiming Eve, they have not known her. They do not know me or my sisters. Deceiving now as with our once first mother by them the dragon wraps another heavy coil upon the captive mind. Ancient liar same. No woman he. Hateful rebel anger fills unnatural emptiness and, using new and former ills, salivates for fruit that is forbidden. The corners of his mouth drip while the serpent in them follows my seed's flesh with lusting old repugnant stare. "My thefts," they say, "if I have any, are my own business."

Not when it's my daughter they are stealing.

"Follow us!" they cry. Athenas who would have my virgin's head and, laughing then, impale her on their shield. Fowlers all and jealous of pure love, devourers, they want hers. They want mine. No more in whispers, now they scream, insisting, weaving false tradition, writhing, they crave our future's flesh and blood and seed. False mothers, twisted sisters chant and call. A new religion whose bad faith denounces as absurd all truth and love and right forever more. Dead eyes, not innocent, blind unopened ones and shut the heart to warnings that a curse doth follow.

Their preying is for her. They want my daughter.

Come first death, I pray thee. Bring swiftly down thy sharpened scythe upon the throat, upon my own arm lest it offend me. But silence them or let this screaming inward river flow away from me, its voice be not heard here anymore. Then would ears of this torn heart no longer know what they would say to one another in the secret place they think they've made. Relieve our eyes of view of all this mural they want to paint. Strength drained and dignity molested, instead of royal purple, now the hooded shroud of shame beveils the would-be woman's face.

Spirit of health or goblin damned?

With slipping eyes decries itself an orphaned child but hungry, seeking refuge, finding falsehood's inner self. A hateful beast seethes beneath the guise. A perfect woman's face, shining and pretentious shy while on her hands first shades of death. Obsessive nervous man flesh in reddish hue from too cropped nails, begins already to creep toward the body. A boy's dry hands. And soon before her time all that was she will be expelled. A man's voice but no man. This not-woman-not-man grasps fair hands that only should a mother's hold and clasps a father's daughter to its breasts. Pretenders! Covenant with hell and death, hooves beat down upon the road. Pale Rider comes.

It comes to take my daughter from her bed, her rest, her children, and her God.

All first nature turns to maggot when revolting false fair skin sends up a fragrant siren. In self-loathe wanton protest they deny the life to our next young whom Heav'n foreordained from their other wombs. Then do not wait to hear the lilting spirit sound of vestal slaves who beg our futures fail that daughters of our flesh might give them answer. False marriage this! Slipped their poison word into her ear, into her heart. Was it so empty then of me? Now a mother's ghost, doomed for a certain term to walk the night and for the day confined to fast in fires till foul crimes done in days of nature are burnt and purged away. Keeping counter vigil on the rampart where in spirit groans she shows the murderous truth to one who cares to look.

Eternal Wisdom goes on weeping, silent to her daughter's ear above those other "mother's" clanging cymbal.

Would anything but deafness by some piercing fever bring sweet relief of silence to the voice of my own flesh and stop my soul from hearing when she calls her? From hearing when she answers? From seeing hateful visions? She wipes the back of her young hand across her mouth, her eyes fixed in liar's glare, and says with those same lips, "I've done no wrong." So promising, that soft pale hand, and in another world one of proverbial wife whose strength upholds the distaff and the spindle, reaching to the poor the lamp whose inner light goes not out even in blackest tempest night. Instead the dry dank breath of abandoned souls, cloud without water, tree twice—dead pulled up by its root, snuffs the candle out. My children's children expire in her kiss and are no more.

When did Judas enter? When did she, as Zeus, this Metis eat?

Sharpened nails unbending, words of reckless iron they loaned her pierce my hands and feet. Icy pressure mounts upon that mantra sounding and with hammer heavy terror falls each time another daughter gives up her voice to theirs and takes the other woman's hand. They are teaching her to steal. They curse and laugh, forswearing that they know not what they do. They mock and part the garment of my life and offer me up vinegar to drink. Coldness owns vacated hearts where abandoned woman sleeps. "Come," says she to my body's fruit. Betraying her true mother, arm in arm with her—they march into the night.

The cave mouth gapes and seethes and down the slippery spiral fool's feet fall.

Can woman vomit up her womb, her soul? Can she expel her breath just deep enough to die or finally close her eyes from mercenary torment? Should true mother's heart be bound, her lips stopped while she be made to watch her own inheritance ask to marry strangers whose inordinate seedless ceremonies counterfeit the marriage of true minds? Must mothers' vigil keep beholding daughters' willing hands extended to caress their foreign gods? Should we accept demands we partner them, the fruit of our own bodies, in dance with Abaddon?

Not one life-giver should. It's not to freedom they would take her.

Anguish mine. My eyes fail not for tears but strain to hold in desperate bonds my first love's last glimpse of mine own offspring's other virgin back until her shape, her voice, her self, her children waiting to be born, and all our destiny, has faded gone, leaving me alone. Sword then to my side, my bowels, my womb, in living dead I cry to her, "Why have you forsaken me?" My life for hers I hang to die without them, my daughter and her daughters. A voice is heard in Ramah. Rachel weeping for her children and refusing to be quiet.

"Come," my last breath whispers after her. "Come back to your borders."

## Christianity: *True* Women's Liberation

Today the paranoia of the secularists runs deep. The blaring light of the religious faith of Christians and the confident culture of life it produces has secularists scrambling about in illogical terror that eclipses the clear and present danger of fanatical Islam. But in many religious circles steeped in dead traditions, the paranoia of the old boys' club runs just as deep and vehement when it comes to women and the issues that concern them.

Modern Christian concept has largely lost its organic connection to the root of Judaism and Jewish life and custom. Contemporary ideals may project a false image of the origin and spread of the faith, particularly in respect to women, thus projecting a model that misses the mark as much as Charlton Heston's portrayal of Moses would be unrecognizable to the actual man who was lifted from the Nile by Pharoah's daughter and met face to face with God on Sinai!

Rodney Stark, one of the world's most respected sociologists of religion, brings valuable light to some of the myths pervading Christian tradition and fueling the fire of opposition to the true faith coming from postmodernists. Regarding the role of women in society and in the church, Stark has produced impressive evidence to prove his claim that Christianity was unusually appealing to pagan women.[4]

One reason for this is that Christian women enjoyed far higher status than did their pagan counterparts. Christianity recognized women as equal to men, children of God with the same supernatural destiny. In addition, the Christian moral code prohibited many of the cultural mores of the pagan culture that threatened the life and health of women. New Testament injunctions against polygamy, divorce, birth control, abortion (often producing death or infertility, perversions of which pro-abortion lobbies now use as argument), and infanticide (usually directed at girl infants) all contributed to the well being of Christian women. New birth into the Kingdom of the Messiah changed the status of women from powerless serfs in bondage to men to valued individuals with dignity and rights of their own in both the Church and the State.

Abortion and infanticide were huge killers of women in this period, but Christian women were spared those horrors. While infanticide, especially of female babies, was a routine and accepted practice among the pagans, the early church forbade it outright. As a result, the Christian subculture did not suffer the enormous shortage of women that plagued the rest of the Greco-Roman world.

In addition, the early church condemned divorce, incest, marital infidelity and polygamy. The earliest church councils prohibited those who married twice from holding office. Pagan religions practiced the old double standard on male and female chastity, as perhaps did Judaism in the time of Christ. Jesus confronted this double standard when religious leaders brought Him a woman practicing sexual immorality.[5] His prescription, we must note, was not only forgiveness and equality, but also repentance. He told the woman, "Go (her release from condemnation and freedom from bondage) and sin no more." Christ required repentance, a basic change of thinking and action on her part in order to walk in the salvation He offered. Christianity demanded virginity from *both* males and females prior to marriage. This was in stark contrast to the pagan culture, where cohabitation was widely practiced and accepted. (As it is in our own day and culture—further proof that the "liberation" philosophy of today's secularists is based on satanic lies and deception.)

Christianity in the beginning, just like God's plan for Eve in the beginning, offered a kingdom where women were valued and empowered as being formed in the image of God. This status afforded them opportunities unavailable to women in the larger pagan society. According to Wayne Meeks of Yale University, "We have already seen that there were a number of women prominently involved in the Pauline circle who exhibited the sorts of status inconsistency which would inspire a Juvenal [a satirical writer in early Roman culture] eloquent indignation. There were women who headed households, who ran businesses and had independent wealth, who traveled with their own slaves and helpers."[6] We have also seen earlier that women played prominent roles of support, influence and leadership in the early church.

Despite the rant and rhetoric of today's women's movement, it is biblical Christianity that provides the true path to liberation for women. Those women who pursue their liberty through the abortion—and lesbianism—glorifying philosophy of the modern women's movement will end up only aborting their own true destiny and identity. It is a choice between a culture of life or a culture of death. We need to choose life and encourage other women to do the same. Life is found in Christ and our destiny is to be formed and prepared as His Bride. It is in the church and the society affected by the true Church moving under the unction and in obedience to the Resident Lord, Holy Spirit that woman's identity and power will be revealed and restored.

In order to release the hidden power of the woman in our generation we must begin and end with God, with what He has ordained and what He intends. As we harmonize with His great power at work in the universe, advancing toward conquest and the end of this present age, we become a point of contact for the power of His salvation. A woman and her faith become the epicenter of a spiritual earthquake, no less than what happened at Jericho, breaking up the age-old foundations of captivity and suppression that have held us and our families in the past.

We stand in Rahab's, window, our faith at work through hope in the power of His blood to be saved from the reckless end of futile thinking and its chaos all around us. Scarlet cord on the wall, we fling wide the door to the *khan* of our hearts and say, "Enter here! *In this inn there is surely room* for you, Sweet Savior!" It is time, as with Rahab, to claim our inheritance. Our house will stand. Our identity will change. And not only ours, but all those we influence!

## Endnotes

1. Ezekiel 28:12,15.
2. Ephesians 4:1, 6-8, 14, 17-24.
3. Matthew 2:18, quoting Jeremiah 31:15.
4. See chapter 5, "The Role of Women in Christian Growth," in Rodney Stark, *The Rise of Christianity*, (San Francisco: HarperSanFrancisco, an imprint of HarperCollinsPublishers, 1996), 95-128.
5. See John 8:3-11.
6. Wayne A. Meeks, *The First Urban Christians: The Social World of the Apostle Paul*, (New Haven: Yale University Press, 1983), 70-71.

# Part Three

## The Hidden Power of the Warrior Woman

# Chapter Six

# Deborah: The "Stinging Bee"

*Give unto the Lord, O you mighty ones, give unto the Lord glory and strength. Give unto the Lord the Glory due to His name; worship the Lord in the beauty of holiness...The voice of the Lord is powerful; the voice of the Lord is full of majesty...The voice of the Lord divides the flames of fire...The voice of the Lord shakes the wilderness; the Lord shakes the Wilderness of Kadesh...and in His Temple everyone says, "Glory!"*[1]

The Presence filled the tent where Lapidoth's family slept. Between wake and sleep just before dawn, his wife sighed and mumbled, as if speaking to the images flashing behind her closed eyelids. Even as the rest of her family slumbered all around her, the rushing Spirit of God came upon her in the customary manner. His tabernacle settled into her very being until Lapidoth's wife was less herself and more a living spirit mingled with the omniscience and power of the Shepherd of Israel.

The Word of the Lord distilled out of his Presence and dropped down like dew, filling her with its weight, its fire budding tiny beads of sweat on her temples. It was bittersweet, this familiar mixture of His Voice and the message the Voice spoke. Not in words of human language so much as understanding and sometimes in images and visions of persons and advance events. At other times she would hear His words addressed to the elders of Israel concerning matters that would come to her for settlement between clans.

Sweet were the messages in the Presence of Him who had made Sarah laugh out loud and made Miriam dance on the shore of the Red Sea. Sweet in the Presence of He Who dwelt in the bush and gave rest to His inheritance under Moses. Sweet as He who opened Heaven's gate and sent down angels when Jacob lay outcast in the wilderness, with only a stone for a pillow. But sometimes they were bitter, as now, as knowledge of the words became clear in her spirit.

In the stillness of predawn this mother of two daughters and three sons lay in fitful half sleep beside her husband. But her visions were not still. Distress and trouble from both above and below swirled about her like the choking incense of strange fire. Amidst the shouts of men and the clash of iron, burning, distress, terror...the burden of Israel settled like a millstone about the neck of her praying soul. Half conscious awareness that Jabin's iron chariots were raiding in neighboring Benjamin crashed in brutal billows with the cries of her people, threatening to take her under for the last time.

*"Awake, Deborah."*

She knew the sound of His voice as well as she knew His name. In her slumber, it always seemed at first as though He was calling from afar. Her spirit rose to meet Him, opening her heart to hear and obey.

As His thick knowing settled into her spirit, this judge of Israel understood that it was time, at last, for war. Israel had once again taken daughters of the land for wives. These pagan women had brought the gods of Canaan with them into the hearts as well as the houses of God's peculiar treasure. "A cake half turned,"

Deborah thought. Israel's faithfulness to YHWH had evaporated like morning dew before the sun. Even in dreamscape, Deborah pondered what it would mean if the fighting reached the foothills or entered the cities where her daughters now lived with their husbands. Curling into a semi-fetal position, she wrapped her arms about her sides as if that would protect the fruit of her womb from harm and prayed against the fateful specter of war.

It was as though the national identity of Israel had unraveled like the threads of worn-out garments from the sanctuary. Their ritual stains too deep to be cleansed, the only use for the once holy coverlets was burning to light the place where *Shekinah* had once dwelt. Deborah clicked her tongue in shame and sorrow. Shiloh was as good as abandoned. Although sacrifices continued in perfunctory preciseness, they drew no reply from heaven.

The heathen nations Israel had failed to dispossess had become a perpetual thorn in her side and smoke in her eyes, just like the smoke from her empty rituals were in the eyes of YHWH. Deep, silent, groans of travail bubbled up from within and passed audibly through Deborah's lips. On the pallet beside her, Lapidoth stirred but did not waken. Unconsciously, his hand reached out in the dark, found hers and she returned his caress. The touch of his hand awakened Deborah fully, and with consciousness, her thoughts found a voice.

"We will have to move the flocks into the caves higher on the mountain range," she said. Lapidoth stirred again. Deborah carefully drew back the blanket that kept the chill of night at bay and rose from the pallet. Feeling about in the darkness, she drew on her seamless woolen outer shirt and silently exited the tent, stepping gingerly between her sleeping sons. From somewhere nearby the trill of songbirds lilted through the predawn night. Deborah listened to their song for a few moments as she gazed at the last twinkling of star splatter on the blue-black dome overhead. As she arranged the long wavy tendrils of her hair into a thick knot at the back of her neck, an involuntary tremor coursed through her body. She did not know whether she shivered against the crisp morning air or because of the new weight of the Voice in her heart.

Yesterday, a runner from the watch posts on Ephraim's mount had reported that five of Sisera's chariots had ransacked a village in Ekron. Two of the farmers had been slain mercilessly as they fled on foot, cut down like so much standing wheat by the curved scythe—like blades wielded by a trio of soldiers aboard one of the dreaded, wheeled, iron, war machines. Laughing all the while, the pitiless marauders cast about crude jests.

"Where is your God now, Hebrew? Now that Ehud and Shamgar are worms' food, who shall save you from our recompense?"

All the village houses were ransacked and then burned. The villagers, armed with nothing more than brooms and shepherds' staves against the might of Jabin's chariots, fled in every direction. Some made it into the nearby hills; many did not. One woman, the unmarried daughter of one of the slain farmers, had disappeared and was still unaccounted for. It was feared that she had been taken by the raiders. Deborah prayed that she was not still alive in their hands.

"Hear O Israel," Deborah sang automatically, her ritual more melancholy than usual, "the Lord our God, the Lord is One." A tear followed the *shema* as her mind's eye filled with images of the unfortunate girl. Her heart wept for that unknown mother who even now was mourning her daughter's fate. She wiped the tear away with her sleeve.

"Elohim, God of our fathers..." Deborah waited for the right words to make her prayer effective. She thought of those who had lived out their lives on this land before her. This land she loved. This earth that gave her meaning of life and knowledge of who she was in the world. Eretz Israel. "Jacob's pillow!" she whispered, "Sweet Cornerstone of Israel, inhabiting heaven and a man's dreams! Light-giver to the stumbler, hear the prayer of Your handmaiden." The angst of her heartache twisted and knotted in her belly. A choked cry came from her throat.

Deborah's mind moved beyond the ravaged village to the plight of her people as a whole. Deep darkness covered the land that had last rested in peace in the days of Shamgar, the shepherd warrior. Her thoughts crystallized on those sleeping peacefully in the tent behind her: Joktan, Ehud and Guel, her sons and Lapidoth, the tower of her heart. It was for them that she prayed. For them she vowed that the iron yokes of Sisera's raiders would be broken off of Israel's shoulders again.

The kings of Canaan were determined to have back the lands that Joshua once half conquered. Sisera would make sure to kill as many Israelites as possible while cowing and beating the rest into submission, exile or tribute. Deborah knew that their own territory of Ephraim was still safe for the moment; their location on the hills overlooking Jezreel was too steep for chariots. But Deborah knew it was only a matter of time. She and Lapidoth spoke of it frequently these days, out of the hearing of their sons' ears. Once the villages on the plains had been laid low, Jabin undoubtedly would lust for the high ground and the vantage offered him by the view of the sea and the trading ships there.

The endless vista before her turned gray with the first hint of light from behind the horizon. Deborah watched as dawn placed her first fiery kiss on the distant hills to awaken the day. A cock crowed. Then the bleating of sheep came to her ears as the ewes in the pens behind the family's sprawling tent were fallen upon by darting lambs with insistent, hungry mouths. Soon Deborah's children would come asking for sheep's milk, too.

Tying her loose clothing around herself, the wick maker stooped down over the fire bed and stirred the coals of yesterday's cook fires. In a moment fresh wood was crackling in the timid blue flames she coaxed out of the warm ashes. As the thin smoke rose toward the heavens, Deborah found her thoughts moving to memories of her father: his rough, earth-stained hands enfolding her tiny ones as she sat on his lap listening to him sing his made up poetry comparing his daughter to the honeybees that tumbled over the yellow petal oceans and explosions of blue irises of the wild flowers of high summer. Without brothers, Deborah had learned to build the fire the same way she had learned to tend and shear sheep—from him.

Lapidoth had been a good arrangement for her. Although the youngest son of his father and thus not the heir, his father's name still meant something honorable in Benjamin. Their two tribes, hers and his, dwelt side by side and shared the border along the road that ran between their two cities. Deborah remembered the vivid stories her father used to tell her of his grandfather's childhood when the ark of God brought them in power as aliens to this land: the tribes arranged in ranks, the trumpeting priests and singers following the armies that followed the cloud whenever God arose. Those were the days when the *shekinah* still dwelt among them.

Lapidoth had taken his bride to Rama where they lived inside the city walls and married away their two daughters into good families. But the security gotten for them by Shamgar when Deborah was still a babe had slipped away as Israel chose new gods. With her parents gone and Israel fragmented according to their regions, Deborah had pleaded with her husband to bring her back here, to the hills of Ephraim, to raise their sons in relative security and grace. But now that too seemed to be slipping away under the threat of this new enemy. She wondered grimly how long Rama would be unmolested and her daughters safe.

Straightening her back and stretching her arms to sift out the ache that had settled there, Deborah rearranged the tumbling heap of linen threads separated from one another through steady, tedious hours of unraveling the stained priests' linen brought to her from the house of God in Shiloh.

Zeal for the sanctuary had been Deborah's vocation since the day she first heard the story of Shamgar. Something in the courage of a man who saw things clearly, whose foundation was the promise of God, who needed no more than his national knowledge of destiny and fear of heaven to subdue an army had taken early hold of her young girl's soul. It was as though the muscled hands of a great unseen Potter had dashed her like a lump of wet clay onto the wheel of His making.

The tale of how one man alone put six hundred of Anak's seed to death with nothing but the ox goad of a farmer had fallen on her ears like a burning coal. That fire had never turned to ash. She dreamed of it as though she had been an eyewitness, even though she was still a small child when she hid behind the curtain in her mother's house, listening while everyone thought she was asleep. She had clutched the curtain over her mouth with her tiny hand to conceal even the sound of her breathing while she listened, enthralled by the story told by men who had come from the fords of Jordan—men who had seen it for themselves. How well she remembered the leaping flames of the hearth fire as it glinted in their eyes and yellowed their faces while they talked.

That night, when she crept back to her pallet and lay down to sleep, the fleeing enemies of Israel ran at her out of the shadows of her dreams. In them valiant Shamgar, beam in hand, served out justice with every heave of his brawny flesh and splintering wood bent against Philistine armor. It was in those dreams Deborah first heard the Voice. He came to her in an omnipotent swirling sense of promise and certainty.

*"I will send My fear before you, and will destroy all the people to whom you shall come; and I will make all your enemies turn their backs to you."*[2]

It was as though she was not herself, the child Deborah, before the Voice. As He spoke in those visions she was Israel, the daughter of God, and all the souls of her people rested in her single trembling heart. Deborah heard the words of God and, later, saw the visions of the Almighty.

> *I will send hornets before you, which shall drive out the Hivite, the Canaanite, and the Hittite, from before you. I will not drive them out from before you in one year; lest the land become desolate, and the beast of the field multiply against you. Little by little I will drive them out from before you, until you have increased, and you inherit the land.*[3]

"So let all Your enemies perish, Lord!" the wick provider said under her breath. A shadow of vehemence flashed across her mouth and melted into softness as the corners of her lips turned up slightly. It was for God that she had been named "stinging bee." After her marriage, little by little, people began to come to her for counsel. More and more the word of her wisdom spread as the Rock of Israel poured out water in her words.

The wife of Lapidoth resumed her work. "Let them that love You be as the rising of the sun in its strength." Her fingers flew along the edge of the discarded priestly robe as she prayed, unraveling its stained threads with practiced ease. Deborah turned her eyes heavenward. It was the dry season in Israel. The land of God languished for lack of rain the way the hearts of the people languished in need of visitation from heaven. With a sigh of sadness, the judge of Israel hugged one knee against herself, resting her chin on its bony mound beneath the layers of wool and linen draped over her lithe frame. Her dark, intelligent eyes looked with fierce love over the wilting landscape before her, and she prayed for rain, first on the hearts of men.

In the distance three figures struggled up the wadi. Too far away to make out their faces just yet, she already knew who they were and why they were coming to sit with her beneath the Two Palms. The tribal chiefs of Issachar had risked their lives to cross the green plain of the valley to the territory of Ehpraim where

Lapidoth pitched his tent between Bethel and Rama. Deborah sat on her rug under the trees that seemed to strut like giant ostriches viewed from a distance. Her palms marked the landscape for miles around while she sat in their shadow twisting wicks for the sanctuary. Already the early morning sun was casting across her carpet long shadows of the jagged palm fronds above her like shadows of the great winged cherubim that hovered over the ark at Shiloh.

In recent days, Deborah's visions had been full of the sighing of the needy and the burden of oppression reigning over the poor of her people in all the territories. Jabin had restored his capital in Hazor, the city of idols. The ark in Shiloh sat silent and without light except for the lamps lit by the wicks Deborah twisted day by day from the stained garments of the priests and piled in heaps around her under the palms. Village life had all but ceased. The pastures that once grazed peaceful flocks were now deserted and her people lived behind the walled defenses of the cities, crowded and hungry with little work, little food and little hope.

The approaching chieftains from northern Palestine represented the tribes of Naphtali, Zebulun, and Issachar. Those tribes whom God had sung His ancient song over:

> Zebulun shall dwell by the haven of the sea; he shall become a haven for ships, and his border shall adjoin Sidon. Issachar is a strong donkey, lying down between two burdens; he saw that rest was good, and that the land was pleasant...Naphtali is a deer let loose; he uses beautiful words.[4]

Deborah could feel the burden of the Lord building against His enemies like water behind a wall. Every day it pressed toward the breakthrough. Recently, she had heard of a valiant man living in Kedesh of Naphtali, in the vicinity of Hazor and Harosheth, the cities of the Canaanites. His name was Barak, "lightning." A man not unlike the Shamgar in her dreams and rumored to be resisting Sisera's army. Barak and his loosely-organized militia of guerilla fighters had stolen the general's horses from under his troops' very noses, pulled the pins of their chariot wheels and left dead men in the wake of their night raids. Lately, Deborah had found herself thinking of Barak more and more often as she sat twisting the wicks for the sanctuary.

It was already late morning by the time the approaching delegation arrived at her place under the Two Palms. Deborah knew already what her answer would be. Lapidoth, two of her sons and the herders had taken the flock up into the high plain to graze. Ehud sat a little ways away from the place where she spread her carpet between the palms and observed as Deborah talked with the men from Issachar who had risked their lives to seek the counsel of God.

Their voices drifted in and out in serious exchanges while Deborah's middle son, by his father's standing order, stayed in sight of his mother in case any of her visitors should become quarrelsome or threatening. If trouble arose too great for Ehud to handle alone, he would summon his father and brothers with the short ram's horn tied to his belt. Mostly, though, it was sheer boredom for the son who drew the lot each day to stay behind while the herders went out on the mountain. Ehud sighed and fiddled with two sticks, occasionally making markings inattentively in the sand around him. At long last it appeared that the men who had huddled in energetic exchange between themselves and his mother were preparing to take their leave.

Their audience over, the visible, hovering flaming fire Deborah was known for gently dissipated and now her countenance no longer shone more than any other woman's. The three men stood, and Issachar's chief spoke for them all.

"The God of Israel keep you, mistress." Then, gathering their water skeins and walking sticks they departed. As they disappeared over the trail leading back to where their donkeys were tied in the shadow of the steppe, Lapidoth came down the lime-stone slope behind the family compound clutching in his fist an untidy bundle of brilliant, red, wild poppies he had found while grazing the flock earlier that morning.

Lost in thoughts of her exchange with the tribal chiefs, Deborah continued unraveling the thread. She was unaware of Lapidoth's approach until a heavy red bloom dropped into her lap—then another and another. When she looked up, Lapidoth was standing over her grinning from ear to ear. Well did he know that these were her favorite of all the flowers that nestled in the moist crannies of the steppe and managed to blossom even in the arid climes between rains. She gathered the red blossoms in her hands.

"Where?" She asked in wonderment. "There's been no rain!" Deborah touched them to her face, smiling as Lapidoth sat beside her.

"My wife gets me favor from on high," he said. Deborah reached out and took his rough herder's hands in her own.

"Yours are the only flattering words that sway me," she said. "And now I should get your food!" Deborah unfolded herself and stood.

Lapidoth's eyes trailed after the diminishing forms of the men who had come to seek counsel from the "wife of torches."

"Is it well with the sons of Issachar?" he asked.

"Not so well," she replied. "The tribes are separated. They even fight with one another along the borders of the territories in their region."

"A divided house with every man doing what is right in his eyes," Lapidoth said grimly. "The lessons of our valiant men before us are mostly forgotten."

"It is God whom Israel forgets, husband."

Deborah bent to gather the pile of twisted wicks and stuffed them into a woven knapsack. She gazed at Lapidoth with reverence and affection. "Would that all of Israel was as you, my lord. A man whose heart is as strong as his back and whose head is as level as the scale of God's justice."

Lapidoth pointed in the direction where the three visitors had gone. "At least the wise still seek him," he said. "Has God spoken to Issachar?"

Deborah nodded. "This morning His Voice came to me."

"It would be good if all the chiefs were such as these," Lapidoth said. "Has the Lord new counsel against the troublers of his people?"

"Only such as confirmed the determinations of those who should know the times and the seasons," she said. "Now they go to Shiloh."

"I was once known in those gates," Lapidoth recalled. "Better a shepherd here."

"They may have trouble," Deborah agreed.

Lapidoth shook his head in sorrow. "All Israel sleeps."

"But I am awake, husband," she sighed. "And the Spirit of God is heavy upon me."

"You must go, then. Did they call you to come with them?"

Deborah laughed. "A woman? The elders in the gates hearken to a wife? In their tradition, a woman's voice is no more than a reed shaken by the wind. You know their saying, "The more maidservants, the more lewdness."

"*Kol isha*, perhaps," he said. "But *bat kol*, daughter of the voice." Lapidoth faced Deborah, admonishing her concerning the burden of God for his nation. "Give, wife," he said. "Give unto the Lord the glory due His name."

Deborah bundled the wicks together. "I shall give the Lord lamps for His sanctuary as I always have," she retorted. "I shall give the people their counsel when they come to me. And I shall give my husband his supper."

Lapidoth watched her as she walked toward the tent. "*Yorah*," he said.

She stopped. The word for the early rain. The warning rain by which the wise prepared for winter. Lapidoth made it a play on the sound of the rain and the sound of Deborah's name. "The day of rain is like the day the law came down on Sinai." He looked at the position of the sun. "We can make Shiloh before they close the gates."

Lapidoth, Deborah and one of their herders, with their donkeys and the bundles of wicks, reached the boundary of the city by mid-afternoon. Dismounting, they entered Shiloh on foot through the "eye of the needle." No sooner were they inside than they heard the sound of raised voices echoing off the stone walls. "It seems God has sent His messengers before His face to prepare the way for the Lord!" Lapidoth said mischievously.

A great calm surrounded Deborah. Her anxiety over the displeasure she expected from the circle of men she was about to meet faded away. Rounding the corner they entered the open stone plaza just inside the gates, the meeting place of the city elders for many legal and business matters. In the center of the plaza, ringed about by the city elders in various postures of attention and repose, stood the three men from Issachar. The one in the center was addressing the elders. It was his voice that Deborah and Lapidoth had heard when they entered.

While still in the shadow of the gate Lapidoth spoke to his wife in a low tone, "Don't be afraid of their faces. These jealous old men comfort the bereaved with one hand while taking bribes against the poor with the other. The best of them builds his own kingdom with no thought of the morrow or of the generations coming after us. It is time they heard from the Lord whom they have forgotten!"

"The tribes are in disarray," the man from Issachar was saying, his hands open toward heaven as he faced the men around him. "There are factions among our own families. The fierce inhabitants of the desert, like locusts in multitude, swarm into the land, a devouring plague. They spread over the country from the Jordan to the Philistine plain!" The man's face was fierce and clear. "Has Shiloh abandoned us? As soon as the harvests ripen they come! We do not even eat of our own labor! When the last of it is gathered they go, having stripped our fields, robbed and maltreated our brethren in every district. And here we sit," he said, indicating the ring of chiefs around the plaza. "Forced to abandon our homes, we congregate in walled cities for refuge!" His companions grunted and nodded their heads in agreement.

Another of the trio from Issachar added, "Sisera's marauders attempt to reclaim the land given us by the God of our fathers. Families are forced to find shelter in caves in the mountains!"

All eyes turned as Lapidoth stepped into the circle. The presiding elder touched his forehead in a ceremonial show of mock respect. "Lapidoth," he said, nodding. Deborah's husband acknowledged the greeting with cool formality. The elder continued, "We assumed you had forgotten that we once went together to the house of God." Eyeing Lapidoth with a steely gaze, he made no effort to disguise his contempt.

Lapidoth met his eyes boldly. "Serpent in a man's skin," he thought. "My flocks keep me in Ephraim these days, Natan."

"Ah, the bleating of sheep," the elder replied. A few of his company laughed. He looked tall Lapidoth up and down. Then, flicking invisible specks of debris from the sleeve and hem of his robes he asked, "What brings you to the city gate today?" He leaned to one side to peer behind the shepherd. "And who hides in your wake, sheep herder?"

Lapidoth's gaze went from left to right across the faces of the influential who sat in ranks aside the presiding chief of the assembly. "I come with a message."

"Message?" the elder replied, his indifference apparent.

"Thus saith the Lord, Natan," Lapidoth said, stepping to one side to reveal his wife standing in his shadow. Taking Deborah by the arm he stood her in their midst and sat down with the men from Issachar.

Some of the circle of men gasped at Lapidoth's astonishing audacity. They knew of the woman many were calling the judge of Israel, but few of them had ever sent for counsel from her except on matters of local territorial disputes among the clans over which she had influence.

Ignoring their hostile eyes, Deborah adjusted her outer garment of brightly colored linen. Its hood resettled around her shoulders like a cloud of glory, reframing her face with an even more striking appearance than she already had. Her face shone with a living radiance.

The presiding elder glared at Deborah with eyes of dull, dead superiority. He had heard of her. *The stinging bee.* Her words had power in certain circles. The men of Shiloh had so far avoided this confrontation. The service she provided bringing the sanctuary lamps had been useful and some of the priests held her in esteem for it. It was allowable for women to seek the counsel of a woman, but too many of the men from the territories, even chiefs like those from Issachar, sought to obey this woman's word. And that was scandalous.

Deborah saw not the men in front of her. Instead, the visions of heaven opened around her. She saw the bema where the Judge of the whole earth sat enthroned as King with the living creatures among the fiery stones and heard choruses of words that human sound could not express. Her being was on the plane of heaven's council, as often happened when she gave her determinations to those who came to the palms in Ephraim.

"Speak up, woman!" the elder snapped. "It goes past the hour for evening repast. Must the drink offering wait for us?"

No longer aware of herself, the Bee exulted in the overwhelming sense of the Presence. It filled her with a bright vehemence. Eyes flashing, dread of judgments against her by this company fled before her face. Like fire welling up, the Voice of the Lord set aflame the ardor of her prayers to God these many months. An ancient flooding spring pushed to break through her lips and overflow onto this company. Her flashing eyes met the dead ones belonging to the presiding chief. But it was not she who looked out through her eyes at him. Deborah heard her own voice dissipate as the sound of the One sitting on glory's throne came into her mouth.

"Wine in golden vessels sours," He thundered. "He who rules over men must be just, ruling in the fear of God. Men whose countenance, as their hearts, are like clear shining after rain. But My house is not so! There is a lion in the streets and the chiefs of My people do not so much as lift a hand to the mouth."

A breeze swirled at Deborah's feet, stirring up tiny whirlwinds of dust. Suddenly the familiar tongues of fire dropped down from Heaven. The liquid fingers of glory appeared and disappeared over Deborah. With them came a sound like the wind in the heavy canvas sails of the merchant ships that ran the trade routes along the coasts. "The Shepherd of Israel spoke by me saying, 'You sit astride white donkeys in robes weighted down with silver! Those to whom the people look for a defense! Your words should drop down like dew upon the branch of Israel, but instead, you have become cisterns that cannot hold water!'"

She spoke to the tribal chief from Dan, whose ships ran cargo for the Amorites, including the iron traded for use as chariot fittings. "Cowing to the tender of the Amorites to maintain his ships, one should not talk while eating lest the food enter the windpipe before the gullet and inflict some deadly injury!"

Lapidoth was smiling slightly. The hair of his arms tingled. He crossed them over his chest in holy self-satisfaction. The authority with which his wife spoke was not her own.

The flood in her words swept away agenda and opinion. Like archer's arrows, a quiver loosed at once, each one was a direct hit in the heart. In the middle of the circle the judge of Israel whirled about. "'Would you build for yourselves paneled houses while My house is fallen into disrepair?' says the Lord."

For a moment some of the men thought they saw a scourge in her hand and wondered how she had hidden it in her robes. They rubbed their eyes. The scourge, like the fiery tongues in the air, seemed elusive. They looked to the chief. Did he see the apparitions?

Gathering her shawl that had fallen in neglected folds around her like the wind—driven dunes of the desert, *the stinging bee* recalled the early words of God in her child's heart. Deborah held an open hand out toward the three men who had come to her between the palm trees. "The men of Issachar declare to you times and seasons! Jabin's commander roves the open land at will, killing, stealing and destroying the daughter of my people, while the chiefs of Israel remove themselves from danger. Village life in Israel has ceased! And those here run down to the sea in ships, making themselves havens in the far inlets out of hearing of the cries of the poor!"

Deborah faced down elder after elder. No modesty softened her as she waited for any one of them to offer reply, to speak, to lead against the iron will of Sisera. Prophetic scenes of the daughter of Ekron flashed before her. Then scenes of her own beloved children. "Has not the Lord said, 'I will drive out the Canaanites from before your face? Only do not spare, do not hesitate to destroy all their idols from your midst lest these people become a perpetual thorn in the side and prick in the eye'? My side aches! My eyes run with tears!" she cried. "The promise was 'If you carefully keep all these commandments which I command you to do...then the Lord will drive out all these nations from before you, and you will dispossess greater and mightier nations than yourselves. Every place on which the sole of your foot treads shall be yours: from the wilderness and Lebanon, from the river, the River Euphrates, even to the Western Sea, shall be your territory. No man shall be able to stand against you; the Lord your God will put the dread of you and the fear of you upon all the land where you tread.'⁵ But the people resort to prayer to the old gods of the land! Even the priests dare to utter the names of idols, double minded that perchance those gods hear or speak!"

Some of those listening to Deborah shuddered. How did she know that they indeed included prayers to idols for help when it seemed YHWH did not answer them?

"Should deliverance rise from dumb stumps and standing stones? Sleepers, awake!" Deborah urged. "Has a nation exchanged its gods, which are yet no gods and my people exchanged its glory for that which cannot profit? Up! For the Lord has given you the land!"

Discomfort tangible in the air filled the open space between the woman and her husband and the rest of the silent assembly. "Where are the fathers of Israel? Instead, the wise men have become silly women, preening and competing in the market-place with one another. Suspicious, following the entourage, each looking to see who wears the finest byssus and sports the newest rings!" The rebuke cut deep. "Hypocrites and thieves!" she said. "Useless hirelings! *Where are the fathers of Israel?*" She spun and pointed directly at the presiding man. "When leaders lead I will praise the Lord!"

This was too much! An outrage! There was nothing custom-ary, nothing acceptable about what this woman from the palms demonstrated before them now. Shock at Deborah's rank demeanor was apparent on the face of every elder. She was, after all, a woman! A woman whose religious zeal raged out of control even of her own husband!

The head of the assembly broke his silence in burning anger. "Woman!" he barked, "Do not flaunt yourself before this assembly!" His lip curled on a tight jaw, his soft thin hands white fisted at her insults. He shot a demeaning look at her husband. "Teach they modesty in Ephraim?" Looking back at Deborah he said, "Let a wife learn to hold her tongue even if no husband dares direct her!" His voice edged higher and higher, his ire screeching until it almost choked away his own sound. "Correct an elder of Shiloh would you? I'll show you power..."

Before he finished, Lapidoth, like a crouching lion about to spring, was halfway on his feet. "You dare threaten the wife of Lapidoth, Natan?" he said through clenched teeth. The fire of holiness that had held them all in check was gone. "My true wife, *lewd?*"

Deborah regarded none of it. She addressed the others in a voice almost inaudible except for the majesty of heaven's glory still on her syllables like so much handwriting on the wall. "If no fathers then, if there is no *man* in Shiloh who dares to stand in the gap against the enemies of Elohim, no one to oppose those who taunt the armies of Israel and mock His covenant night and day then..." Deborah stood erect, her feet apart on the stone plaza. "*I* will arise! *A mother in Israel!*" With that she turned and took two steps toward the gate. Her hand went out and touched Lapidoth's shoulder briefly as she passed, grateful for his faithfulness and courage. He covered her hand with his. With no more than a nod to the men of Issachar, Lapidoth and Deborah left the gate.

The Presence that went out with her was like a passing thunderstorm, drenching the garments of pride around the elders like men caught in the open fields. The elders shuddered. The cold weight of the unexpected cloudburst that came by the shepherd's wife stunned them to silence. For a few moments the circle of the council was immobilized under the weight of her words. A discordant quiet, the charred remains of their pomp and self-satisfaction sagged like wrecked sails among the shipyards. A creaking vacancy stalked the blackened timber of their indolence towards Israel's national destiny.

No one of this old company rushed to speak. Reasoning in their hearts, man after man among them considered his own defense and some of them simply dismissed her. A few uneasy ones fidgeted for the first opportunity to exit. Eyes slipped from side to side, their glances briefly meeting and slipping askance to avoid cold stares. The shallow facade of their brotherhood had been broken and stripped away to reveal the hollow emptiness underneath.

The eldest among them rose up at last. "The day is late and certain matters adjure me elsewhere. Prayers and livestock demand my strength before shabbat's command." With a stiff bow the dark, sharp-featured man gestured, touching a hand lightly to his forehead and chest. The rest of the company began gathering themselves together. All were struggling to find the words to express their anger and discomfiture.

"Smoke and vinegar, this wife of torches!" someone said. "Her demeanor blunts her discernment!"

"Or any chance the discerning should give ear to her advice!" another said. "She should study Miriam's fate! Leprosy put her outside the camp for as much as this!"

"And there she would have remained had not merciful Moses interceded. Offer an intercession at evening prayers," someone suggested. "Perchance God will show mercy and grant her repentance. Her husband seems beyond himself in her power."

Several of the others coughed and nodded in agreement.

"He should keep his house in order to get any honor here," the presiding elder said, his religious tone deepening. "If the serpent bites because the charmer withholds his gift, then no preference be given that man."

A wavering chorus of "aman!" lifted off the lips of those who remained.

"This is no sister of Aaron," one man added. "Why would she take audience in the open air of the palms except she had need to allay opinions of her character?"

Heads nodded. "Good reason, brother."

"I saw the flames!" another said. "Did not our hearts burn?"

"How did she know the workings inside the inner sanctum?" another asked suspiciously. "A woman cannot enter there! What strange manner of sight is this?"

"Witchery perhaps," one man gasped.

Then a young chief from Rueben spoke. "Since the days of Shamgar there has been no match for Jabin's army. Strength of the ancients lay not in their own arm but in the right hand of God when He was pleased to favor them." He paused. "I saw the flames, too. And I heard the sound in her voice. A voice like the voice of the Lord." He looked from eye to eye. "Like mustering armies. I felt it within. The hosts of heaven preparing for war."

"The voice of spirits from an arrogant wife. Should not the tribes of Israel seek their chiefs for counsel?" the presiding chief demanded.

"Should not the chiefs of Israel seek the counsel of God?" the Ruebenite countered.

"Counsel of a woman?" someone else shot back. "Flaunting, presumptuous ewe!"

But Rueben had not relented yet. "Had we no mothers? Do we not give them honor?"

"If it be from God her counsel will stand. If not..." the man from Dan said.

"If not," one of the elders of Simeon put in, "we continue to live in rocks and caves. We must consider this matter more carefully!"

"Brethren!" the presiding elder was forced onto his own feet. "See how she draws our entire attention and entices us to disassemble! Proof enough of what power she exercises. *"Flames? Burning?* Pure seduction! *Kol isha.* Has not God said, *"Because you hearkened to Kol isha, the voice of your wife, damned be the soil for your sake?"*

Several immediately agreed.

He cleared his throat surreptitiously, leaning to the scribe sitting aside him. The scroll open and blank, the scribe looked helpless. "Send for Lapidoth after the new moon. Call him alone. Without the skirts of his wife as a tent. He shall answer for this or his name will be as a mute man in Israel."

In three days Deborah sent for Barak. They sat together under the palms, Deborah's son a little distance off as before while his mother spoke with the warrior of Naphtali.

"Lightning flashes, but rain waters the earth," the guerilla fighter told her. "The coffer holds the tablets, the manna and Aaron's rod that budded. But the *shekinah* that goes before burns up all our enemies. Where is the glory of Israel now? Jabin fattens himself, continuing in his capital unmolested. Sisera mounts the iron chariots, holding the southern boundaries and annexing our tribes. A house divided in strength. At least in my own territory, we resist the son of Belial."

"More strength is required of the axe man when the blade is blunted," Deborah argued.

"The smithy of the nations dulls the blade of Israel day by day," Barak shot back. "Why should I leave my own clan defenseless to take up the cause of the tribes who will not protect themselves?"

"Jabin strikes the anvil perhaps," Deborah replied. "But there is One who made the smith." She met Barak with her gaze. Could she have but seen it, the glint of fire in her eyes was the same as that she remembered in the eyes of the messengers who had told Shamgar's story in her mother's house so long ago. "Up, Barak. I have seen it in the night visions. Has not the Lord said, 'Draw toward Tabor?'"

The commander's face flushed with recognition of the words of the prophecy. On the heights, as the sun broke over the valley floor before the mists of the night had burned off, Barak had heard the Voice of the Shepherd of Israel for the past seven days. "*Up, Barak!*" the Voice had said.

The prophetess folded back the corner of her rug and grasped one of the hooks that held her hair, letting her long tendrils fall around her like a veil. She wrote on the ground with the hook's sharpened end. "See here, call ten thousand from your kinsmen and from the men of Zebulun. Gather them in Tabor." She marked the mountain as a triangular peak with an "x" atop it. "From there you have the high ground. Send spies to spread the word that Israel musters a rebel force in Ephraim. Sisera's pride will draw him as a fishhook in the jaw of Leviathan. He will come up to you in the foothills between the mountain and the river."

Barak studied the sand drawings as Deborah made the curving snake of the river Kishon bordering the round wheels repressing Sisera's iron chariots. He took the hook from her hand, taking over the battle plan from his own knowledge of the terrain. The fire in his belly urged him on, stirred up since he had first heard the *bat kol* in the early dawn.

"The rocky terrain will force his captains from their chariots and they will have to split up to follow my men into the hills. The sons of Naphtali, whose legs are like the hinds on the high places, are surefooted in the terrain that has reared them from youth."

Deborah smiled her slight smile. "The blessing of the Almighty!"

"Not a man of them will escape our sword. The wilderness of Kedesh shakes with the sound of His strength, as you have said."

Barak's words were a prayer and a vow in one breath. He looked at Israel's judge, the woman of flames. "You will come with us."

Deborah shook her head. "A wife among the troops? The tongue-waggers already have enough fuel to burn the forests of Lebanon. If you take a woman it will be a woman's name, not Barak's on the lips of the balladeers after this."

Barak studied her markings in the sand. "You have the victory here, Wick-weaver," he said, tapping his heart, "as much as I have it in my head." The commander poked the drawing with her hair hook. "It's victory, not fame I crave," he said flatly, "whatever hands God gives it through. Besides, if the men of Israel are as valiant as you expect, who among them would dare to stay behind at home while even a woman rises up against Israel's enemies? Like the cloud that once traveled before the coffer, I will not go unless you go with me."

"Up! Barak! Draw ten thousand to Tabor. For the oppression of the poor, and the sighing of the needy," the judge of Israel said at last. Her wisp of a smile tugged the corners of her mouth and the fire—glint of Shamgar shone in her eye. "Now God will arise. The Sanctuary of Israel will bless His people with security." Deborah swiped the marker away from the warrior and stuck it into the sand in the midst of Jabin's chariots drawn there. "And iron sharpens iron," she laughed. "Your legend belongs to a woman now!"

## Endnotes

1. Psalm 29:1-2, 4, 7-8, 9b.
2. Exodus 23:27.
3. Exodus 23:28.
4. Genesis 49:13-15b, 21.
5. Deuteronomy 11:22-25.

# Chapter Seven

# The Voice and the Glory

According to the sages, Israel experienced the Voice of the Lord in two ways, the supreme experience of which was the dual manifestation of the spirit of prophecy accompanied by a miraculous manifestation in natural elements. Thus God's voice was both seen and heard. The first appearance of the Voice of God in this manner, with two great witnesses, is at creation, "in the beginning." God spoke into the cloud of His rushing Spirit, Who hovered over the elements in chaos as an eagle over her nest. Words and elements came together in the power of the Spirit, and creation came into being.

Likewise, the Voice and the pillar of fire came together for Moses at the burning bush and again later on Sinai when he received instruction to lead and mold Israel. The Voice of the Lord was accompanied by the *shekinah*, the glory of God that rested over the tabernacle and ultimately filled the temple with God's manifest presence, accompanied by miracles.

Jesus, Who was with the Father working in the beginning, resumed His work on earth, when He came as the second Adam, giving the Word and confirming it with miracles. The Father, Son and Spirit worked together to bring light into the darkness and peace into the chaos that reigned through sin. Thus men *"beheld His glory"*[1] in their midst. These "two witnesses" manifested together—Word and wonders—confirmed that the Voice and the message were those of the immutable God.

A secondary manifestation of the Voice of the Lord was purely the spirit of prophecy resting on a vessel of God's choosing, not always a particularly consecrated vessel (such as Balaam and King Saul) and not necessarily human (such as Balaam's donkey). The spirit of prophecy was expected to be judged by the hearers. Unfortunately, they often "heard" wrong, such as after Jesus' baptism, when some said it thundered, thus rejecting the Word of the Lord.

The Voice alone, without the miracle of nature, was known as *bat kol*, the daughter of the Voice. Even then it was expected to rest primarily upon holy men. *Bat kol* is seen upon the prophets and judges of biblical record. At their word, the people of God were delivered, chastised or given strategic command. The major and minor prophets of Scripture were vessels of *bat kol*. These encounters were an advent of the Holy Spirit, light in the midst of darkness, the result of the Israel's adultery with the gods of the pagan cultures surrounding them. Even during those times, as we see throughout the history of God and man, He left them with His Voice if they would hear. Such were the times when Deborah arose to judge Israel.

During times of apostasy, the Voice of the Lord rested in human vessels called "judges" in the Bible. The judges were a combination of prophet, priest and warrior and included a woman in their company. Deborah, the wife of Lapidoth, judged Israel during one of its darkest periods of national crisis.

By the second generation of those who entered Canaan under Joshua's command, the priesthood set forth by Moses was practically nonexistent. The Voice of the Lord and the miracles of power confirming His word departed from the tent of meeting to rest in the spirit of prophecy on leaders chosen of God. Prior to this, the high priest received answers to weighty community matters and issues of national destiny through the prophecy of the stones on the breastplate. Hidden in the "heart" of the ephod, the Urim and Thummim spoke to Israel on all matters from A to Z! To these Israel's kings and military commanders came for strategy in war. But when the priesthood was in malaise, God raised up those who would give unto the Lord the glory due His name just as Psalm 29 commands. Such was the anointing upon Deborah.

One of the most painful circumstances in the history of the judges is the utter silence that seems to envelop Shiloh and its sanctuary during this time. No help comes from the priesthood until quite near the close of this period. Far away in Mount Ephraim God raised up a woman on whom was the Voice or the spirit of prophecy. The sacred text conveys that Deborah exercised her gift in strict accordance with divine law, not for her own purposes but as a judge of Israel:

> Now Deborah, a prophetess...was judging Israel at that time. And she would sit under the palm tree of Deborah between Ramah and Bethel in the mountains of Ephraim. And the children of Israel came up to her for judgment.[2]

She was "the wife of Lapidoth," which in Hebrew also reads, "the woman of flames." This reminds us of the appearance of the shekinah, which overshadowed the ark and went before Israel to give them victory. All in Israel who sought judgment at her hands met her between Ramah and Bethel, under a palm tree that afterwards bore her name. The fact that Deborah moved heaven and earth and her power of prophecy was accompanied by signs and wonders ranks her alongside Moses, father and lawgiver, as a female lawgiver as well as a mother in Israel.

## A Legacy of Prejudice

However, this ancient female judge is the one woman, besides Jezebel, *never* venerated by ancient Judaism in the generations after her time. While Rahab and Tamar are exalted as examples of womanly virtue, the judge Deborah was regarded as an arrogant aberration not to be emulated. They decried her, citing her words, "Until I, Deborah arose," as proof of her pride. They impugned her reputation by twisting her practice of meeting visitors under a palm tree to imply that she had to "hold court" in public in order to avoid accusations of lewdness. Centuries later, in a thinly veiled play on the spelling of Deborah's name, a religious proverb about men who put faith in the witness of a cat and a well was created to besmirch her without coming right out and saying so verbatim.[3]

But God is faithful to Himself, to His promises, to His covenants and to His purpose for mankind. Like a river, the Holy Spirit flows around those who oppose Him and finds His way to the lowly and oppressed through vessels who are willing to be His messengers. History shows that the Holy Spirit holds some affinity for using women as messengers, witnesses, and vessels of victory, particularly in times of crisis and history making. His example of Deborah stands in direct testimony against ancient taboos and traditions of prejudice against women wielding natural authority and spiritual power within their culture.

Deborah was one of seven prophetesses recorded in Scripture: Sarah, Hannah, Deborah, Miriam, Esther, Abigail, and Hulda. We have already visited Sarah and God's admonition that Abraham "Hearken to the voice of his wife." We will see in a later chapter that the voice of Abigail was used to direct the actions of David, future King and ancestor of the coming Messiah. Perhaps the least known of these women prophets, however is Hulda, whose account is recorded in 2 Kings 22:8-20.

*Then Hilkiah the high priest said to Shaphan the scribe, "I have found the Book of the Law in the house of the Lord." And Hilkiah gave the book to Shaphan and he read it...Then Shaphan the scribe showed the king, saying, "Hilkiah the priest has given me a book." And Shaphan read it before the king. Now it happened, when the king heard the words of the Book of the Law, that he tore his clothes. Then the king commanded Hilkiah the priest, Ahikam the son of Shaphan... "Go inquire of the Lord for me, for the people and for all Judah, concerning the words of this book that has been found; for great is the wrath of the Lord that is aroused against us, because our fathers have not obeyed the words of this book, to do according to all that is written concerning us. So Hilkiah the priest, Ahikam, Achbor, Shaphan and Asaiah went to Huldah the prophetess, the wife of Shallum the son of Tikvah, the son of Harhas, keeper of the wardrobe. (She dwelt in Jerusalem in the Second Quarter.) And they spoke with her."[4]*

Due to the king's swift repentance and reforms, it is evident that the portion of the Law Shaphan read to the king was from Deuteronomy, outlining the judgment and curse to come on Israel if she turned from the ways of the Lord. Distraught, the king sends the men to inquire of the Lord. According to the sages, "Jeremiah prophesied in the marketplace, Zephaniah in the houses of worship and Hulda to the women." It is also likely that Nahum and Habakkuk were also ministering in and around Jerusalem at this same time. So why, if all these "great male prophets" were at the king's disposal, did he send the high priest go to the "women's prophet"?

According to Leah Kohn in her study of women in Judaism, it was precisely because she was a woman that the king consulted Hulda: "Simply stated, the Talmud (Megillah 14b) tells us that 'women are more compassionate than men,' and this is the quality king [Josiah] sought from Hulda."[5] He knew that the no matter what vessel the Word of the Lord came through, the message would be the same. But he also knew that the tone and delivery of the message would be shaped by the one who gave the word. She continues:

> Hulda's tone of mercy is what differentiates her delivery of Hashem's message from those [Josiah] might have received from the men. Hulda's prophecies contain a feminine tone of nurturing, sensitivity and compassion. These are the qualities behind the Talmudic citation that, "women are more compassionate than men." Hulda gives the king the encouragement and hope he needs in order to eradicate idolatry from the Temple. Her prophecy inspires the king, and perhaps the entire Jewish Nation to repent. Her memory and the significance of her presence are ultimately memorialized in the "Gates of Hulda" seventy years later, with the rebuilding of the Second Temple.[6]

Thus, it was precisely the feminine nature that God used to usher in what was the greatest national revival in Israel's history. In direct opposition to criticism concerning Deborah, that it was to shame Israel for apostasy that God used a woman to judge and lead the people into battle, Hulda was a chosen vessel of the Voice at a time when there were several godly and righteous men at the forefront of ministry. Hulda is evidence of God's plan to use the voice of women, utilizing the innate qualities of her femininity to deliver His message in these last days.

Both Hulda and Deborah were women who understood and walked in submission to God and righteous authority. We see this first in the description of the women given in Scripture: Deborah is described as, "the prophetess, wife of Lapidoth"; and Hulda, in addition to her relationship to her husband and his family back three generations, is described practically down to her street address! Both women are identified relationally, by their place in their community and their recognized role contributing to the fabric of their society. This is a characteristic of anyone, man or woman, who desires to walk in authority: we are to be integrated into a community where we are firmly planted and recognized to be under authority. Others should be able to look at us and know to whom we are related. Even Jesus, when He began His earthly ministry was known by His relationships and was publicly ordained in the waters of baptism when the Father spoke and said, "This is My Beloved Son, in whom I am well pleased."[7]

Biblical submission is harmonious obedience and service to the purpose and will of God. This is why submission to godly authority becomes a weapon for the kingdom of light. It is also why assuming a servant spirit, as Jesus did when He clothed Himself in human flesh, becomes the channel for change even in situations where those in authority are unrighteous: "He humbled Himself and became obedient to the point of death, even the death of the cross."[8] At the same time, however, Jesus did not lay down before the false traditions and religious spirits of the day; He followed the will and purpose of God.

The Church's understanding of submission, like the evolution of religion, with each generation moving farther away from direct visitation by God, has been distorted, forming and retreating to devised traditions of man. Generally, women have been the ultimate losers, except when revival hits and the Holy Spirit falls upon God's handmaidens.

## Handmaiden—Warrior of God

One of these handmaidens, and perhaps the most remarkable and well known outside the Bible, was Joan of Arc. Widely revered as the national heroine of France, this young 15th-century woman grew up in circumstances not wholly unlike those that Deborah faced in her day. Joan enters the stage of history in the middle of the event known as the Hundred Years War. France in the early 1400s was a divided nation. Defeated and subjugated by England, in 1420 France signed the Treaty of Troyes granting England's King Henry V ascension to the throne of France upon the death of her current monarch, the mad Charles VI.

Unexpectedly, however, both Charles VI and Henry V died in 1422, leaving Henry's infant son, Henry VI as king of both England and France. This meant that, effectively, no one occupied the French throne. Conditions for the French people were grim. Children died of starvation by the thousands. Lawlessness and immorality were rampant. Many people lived barely above the level of their animals. Charles VII, the original heir to the French throne who had been cut off by the Treaty of Troyes, was unable to successfully press his claim to the kingship.

It was into this chaotic state of national peril that young Joan appeared. Illiterate and with no training in the doctrines or theology of the church, Joan nevertheless possessed a deep and abiding love for God. Furthermore, from the age of 13 she had been receiving visions and hearing "voices" that gave her spiritual guidance; voices she later identified as Michael the archangel and two early Christian martyrs, St. Catherine of Alexandria and St. Margaret of Antioch. However we might interpret such voices today, Joan was convinced that her voices—and their message—came from God.

By 1428, when she was 16, Joan had received visions of horses in battle and herself leading an army of men. Joan trusted God completely and became convinced that He was leading her to go to the aid of Charles VII. Her first attempt a month later to offer her services to the commander of Charles' army was rebuffed with contempt. Imagine a *girl* leading troops against the enemy!

Joan returned home, but her voices were insistent. In October, just a few months later, France stood on the brink of total collapse when the English attacked the city of Orleans. Heeding once more the urgent call of her voices, Joan offered her services a second time. This time, however, through a series of divinely ordained events she was able to convince the army commander and the embattled king not only of her sincerity but also of the divine nature of her mission. She held her own in a one—on—one contest in swordsmanship with the army commander and answered for the king three personal questions that were known only to him and God. Later, she was examined by a committee of theologians and church officials. Not only did this illiterate teenager stand up to their questions, but they also accepted her claims of supernatural guidance.

Divine insight carried Joan at every turn:

Returning to Chinon, Joan began preparing for her campaign. It was at this early stage that two significant events occurred that appeared to confirm even more the divine nature of her mission. Joan needed a sword, and she knew where to find one. She wrote to the priests at the chapel of St. Catherine of Fierbois, informing them that her sword was buried behind the altar. Indeed, the sword was found at that exact spot.

The second event involved a letter, which still exists, written on April 22, 1429, and delivered and duly registered before any of the events referred to in the letter took place. The writer of the letter reported that Joan had said that she would deliver the city of Orleans; she would compel the English to raise the siege; she herself would be wounded, but would survive; and Charles would be crowned king before the end of the summer. As it turned out, all of these things were fulfilled just as Joan predicted.[9]

When Joan arrived on the field and announced her mission to the battle-weary French soldiers, her presence, piety, holiness and devotion had an effect that could only be called supernatural. These coarse, vulgar, immoral and demoralized soldiers flocked to Joan's banner in droves. At her insistence, they even cleaned up their language and behavior! Even though wounded in the process, Joan did indeed lead them to victory. Orleans was saved, the English were routed, and on June 17, 1429, Charles VII was formally crowned king of France.

The war continued, despite this great victory, and the following summer Joan was captured while defending the city of Compeigne from the Burgundians. The French king Joan had served so faithfully did nothing to help her and her captors sold her to the English, who were desperate to get their hands on her. The English were determined to have her life in return for the embarrassment they had suffered on the battlefield at her hand. But their defeat in battle was insufficient grounds for executing her. Instead, they put her on trial for heresy. Throughout the months of proceedings, designed to wear her down with intense and hostile questioning by church leaders, Joan's faith and purity stood forth unshaken, a fact attested to by the official records of her trial, one of the most thoroughly documented events of that time.

In the end, Joan was condemned to death, not for heresy but for the "crime" of wearing men's clothes. On May 30, 1431, she was burned at the stake. Some years later, Joan's condemnation and execution were officially repudiated and her reputation was restored. In 1920 the Catholic Church canonized her as St. Joan of Arc. Like Deborah before her, this handmaiden of God heard and followed the Voice arose as a warrior to restore and defend the destiny of nation.

## Male *and* Female: God's Kingdom Order

Against all human logic and human odds, Joan of Arc was victorious. She did not succeed because she *heard* the Voice but because she *obeyed* the Voice. It was the same way with Deborah, with one major exception: Deborah would have never succeeded without the help of Barak. And Barak would never have succeeded without Deborah. Victory required the two of them working together in harmony. This in itself was an echo of how things were originally designed in Eden.

In fact, in every way the triumph of Deborah and Barak exemplifies the triumph of God in perfect kingdom order. Under the unction of the Holy Spirit in a *kairos* moment, these two formed a perfect partnership in the anointing between male and female. They represent what God desires to do to bring about successful leadership particularly, but not exclusively, in times of distress and crisis. Although Deborah and Barak were not husband and wife, their co-laboring, each adding to the other what God gave them grace to supply, provides a perfect picture of what God intended when He made mankind *male and female* in the beginning.

Deborah and Barak also demonstrate what can be accomplished in a marriage between equally yoked partners who are committed to the purpose of God in their generation. Marriage uniquely presents the opportunity of a lifestyle of spiritual success between partners who are filled with the Spirit of God and led by Him! Barak was not sufficient in courage or strategy without Deborah as his helper/counterpart. Neither did Deborah presume to go on her own but instead gave herself fully to the anointing and the Voice of the Lord, realizing she had come to the kingdom for such a time as was at hand. But together they made beautiful music! Together they got the victory!

This is exactly what God intended when he formed Eve out of the side of the first human, Adam, and brought her to him as the helper fit for him. We must also realize that God the Holy Spirit is the key to this harmony and wisdom. Deborah's motherhood was for her nation. There is nothing more terrible to deal with than a faithful mother whose children are being threatened! Such was this woman's patriotism towards the nation that birthed her. There was nothing and no one who would stand in the way of victory when she went to war for the destiny of Israel.

Wielding authority in the manner of Elijah and Daniel, she rallied angelic hosts and the very elements of nature to her side.[10]

Deborah's name, "bee" indicates the double-edged sword of the Word of the Lord on her tongue: sweet and fertile as pollen to make the planting of the Lord fruitful, and sharp and divisive as a sting to administer justice where there is no righteousness.

The empowerment of Deborah embodies the significance of a woman overshadowed by the Holy Spirit and completely under His hand of power. In these days that we live in, the true prophetic unction resting upon and released within women will be a critical key to God's victory strategy. Deborah the prophetess, the woman of flames in whom was the Voice of the Lord, was the first woman prophet/leader to arise after the law was handed down. She is a *prima facie*, the "first face" of what Joel later prophesied about God pouring out His Spirit on all flesh. Realized at Pentecost, divided flames of fire sat on each believer (male *and* female) in that upper room and they all prophesied. The Voice and glory that were lost to man and woman at the fall were restored at Pentecost!

As we move closer to the appearing of the Bridegroom, the bride is making herself ready; that is, men and women, His menservants and His maidservants, leading *together* as one to show forth the image and glory of God. The Father is keeping the promise He made to the first woman: "Your seed shall crush the serpent's head"! As the power of the woman is hidden no longer, we shall hear the Spirit and the bride, men and women co-laboring together, saying, "Come!" God has kept His covenant with Eve. He is restoring her voice!

## "You're in My army now!"

Jennifer is one woman who has heard the Voice and found her own restored. It happened at one of our conferences. Her experience reminds us of the Scripture that says, "Blow the trumpet in Zion, and sound an alarm in My holy mountain! Let all the inhabitants of the land tremble; for the day of the Lord is coming; for it is at hand."[11] She describes the transformation that occurred in her encounter in this way:

The first time I attended an MCM conference, in 1998, I had a very supernatural encounter with the Lord. I went home after the Friday night session and fell asleep. I was awakened suddenly by a very, very loud shofar trumpet blast. I wasn't very familiar with a shofar at this time but had only seen one someone had brought back as a souvenir (so I thought) from Israel. I shot up in the bed, stunned. The sound was full of many sounds...a mighty waterfall, a trumpet blast, a mighty wind. I thought my alarm clock had gone off accidentally. It hadn't. As I turned to check it, I noticed that the time was exactly 3:00 A.M. Suddenly, I heard an audible voice speak, saying, "Get your boots on! You're in My army now!" It was the voice of the Lord, very authoritative yet very gentle at the same time. Then I had an open vision of myself in a wedding dress with black combat boots on.

This experience shook me to the very core of my being. I was not in church and had not been to church for several years. But I knew I had to be obedient and heed this literal call from God to get to church to worship and pray. I knew in that instant that I was called to All Nations Church. The minute I walked in the door the Holy Spirit said, "You're home now." And that's where I've been ever since.

In the years since, God has taken the rubble of the mess I had made of my life and has faithfully rebuilt me layer by layer. Like the Bride in Isaiah 54, he has transformed me: "Behold, I will lay your stones with colorful gems, and lay your foundations with sapphires. I will make your pinnacles rubies, your gates of crystal, and all your walls of precious stones." My life will never been the same.

## A Woman Shall Encompass a Man

God's plan in creation was for man and woman to work together in harmony as perfect and equal counterparts, each complementing the other in exercising dominion over the created order. Marriage is a visual picture of this relationship. Paul described marriage between a man and a woman as a picture of Christ and His eternal bride, the Church.

Revelation 21 depicts the Lamb's wife as the new Jerusalem coming down from God adorned for her husband. A city is a perfect illustration of the woman in all her glory: a secure, permanent center of provision, security, identity and community, full of industry; the "good wife" of Proverbs 31, with her surrounding wall of governmental jurisdiction, into whose embrace one comes for life. God is the founder and builder of that city. From the side of Adam, God formed woman in His image and built her together to reflect His glory.

In our generation, God is adding the final touches to her perfection. We are witnesses of the unfolding promise made to Eve in the garden. As the history of the world approaches the close of the age, the hidden power of the woman God made is coming full circle. As the prophet Jeremiah said, *"For the Lord has created a new thing in the earth—a woman shall encompass a man."*[12]

The "new thing" Jeremiah foretold is the old thing God promised Eve in Eden: "Your seed shall crush his head." This first promise given to woman as life giver and mother of all the living indicates that she has been given divine ordination to be a vessel whose influence and participation in any seed-bearing endeavor should produce greater good than was possible without her.

There is no fatherhood without a woman involved. This truth applies to the very foundation of the Church called to be a light and embassy of the Kingdom of Heaven on earth. One of the heretical religious traditions that has come down through the ages is the exclusion of the woman from spiritual authority and ministry on the basis of her gender. We find no example of God setting forth this pattern on earth or in His heavenly kingdom. It is rather a development of assumption and the influence of sin in societal and religious culture which relegates woman to a position of inferiority to man.

When God told Eve her husband would rule over her because she ate the forbidden fruit and persuaded him to do so as well, and when God told Adam he would suffer because he had "listened to the voice" of his wife, He was not indicating her gender. He later told Abraham, the father of our faith, to "listen to her voice" when Sarah demanded he exile Hagar and the illegitimate heir.

Judeo-Christian taboos against women stem from an anti-feminine attitude which sages developed over centuries, beginning under Judaic law—and which some of the early church fathers inherited from the Greco-Roman culture in which they grew up. The serpent that seduced Eve in the garden has gone after Adam through religious rituals but his plan is still the same: silence the voice of the one foretold to embody satan's defeat!

Once again, the natural ordinances of the law were given as a shadow to point to Christ, the husband of humanity, who would come as the second Adam in a human body to taste death physically while remaining sinless, and triumph over sin and death for humanity's sake in His resurrection. Thus He "fulfilled the law" of God written in human ordinances.

The triumph of Calvary fully applies to the woman. Unfortunately, we cannot overlook the fact that although the message of Christianity has been consistent with this truth linguistically, the traditions relating to and the experience of women generally have not reflected full redemption from the curse. This is not God's doing, but as He told her in the beginning, "Your desire shall be for your husband," (all those things you may long for, need and experience as a woman in a mortal body) "and he shall rule over you" (you will be the slave of what mortal man can muster)!

Like Eve in the garden after she ate, creation has been subjected to the command and now wrestles against sin and death in hope of full redemption in the One who was to come.[13] Still bringing forth the same life for which she had been created, albeit now thru much pain and sorrow, woman has waited until such a time as the Seed she travailed to bring forth would crush the opposition and restore her to her former glory together with her husband and to God as she was before when perfection and glory clothed her and she walked with God and the man in power.

The Seed has come. He has crushed the head of enmity. She and all creation are *"delivered from the bondage of corruption into the glorious liberty of the children of God."*[14] Yet the doctrine of sin has been exalted above the Seed that destroyed it. Christ has restored woman and now offers by the Spirit the power for her to rule over the sin that sought to claim her destiny in the beginning. Her time has come and Her Bridegroom who bore that burden will unveil her, a mystery of man and woman nourished by Him as His own body. This completed work shall reveal woman as a helper fit to rule and reign beside Him on His throne. Let them love. Let them live. Let them lead!

As the hidden power of God emerges in the woman who fully follows Christ, get ready for empowerment in the church, redemption in society, miracles in the body and blessings on the human race unequal to any generation previous! The Voice and the glory have been restored! We say "Come Holy Spirit! In truth and in power overshadow us!" Together with the Spirit we say, "Come, Lord Jesus! Come out and meet Your wife!"

## Endnotes

1. John 1:14.

2. Judges 4:4-5.

3. In Vol. VI., p. 64, of the periodical *Hakol* Michael L. Rodkinson explains the significance of this proverb: "It is entirely unreasonable to assume that one could believe in a cat or a well otherwise

than as a means by which God would punish an iniquity, and therefore it is highly probable that the words 'Huldah and Bor, meaning *cat* and *well*, originally were intended for 'Huldah and Deborah, the prophetesses of the Scriptures, and that simply a Daled and a Heh were omitted in the manuscript. The Talmud generally treats prophetesses with but little consideration and regards their prophecy as of small value, for it says in Tract Megilla, p. 37, 'Greatness is not seemly for women. Two prophetesses we had and one was called Deborah (a bee) and the other 'Huldah (a cat).' It then continues to criticise their behavior in general; but still the King Yoshiyahu (Josiah) believed in 'Huldah the prophetess (see II Kings, xxii. 13 to 20) and Barak the son of Abino'am believed in Deborah (see Judges, iv. 8). Thus it would be far more reasonable to explain the above passage in the Gemara, not with reference to the cat and the well, but rather as referring to Deborah and 'Huldah, and say: If a man have faith in the prophetesses 'Huldah and Deborah, he should be so much the firmer in his faith in God."

4. 2 Kings 22:8-14.

5. Leah Kohn, "Women in Judaism," Project Genesis Inc.

6. Ibid., Leah Kohn, "Women in Judaism," Project Genesis Inc.

7. Matthew 3:17.

8. Philippians 2:8.

9. Michal Ann Goll, *Women on the Frontlines: A Call to Courage*, (Shippensburg, PA: Destiny Image Publishers, 1999), 37.

10. Judges 5:20.

11. Joel 2:1.

12. Jeremiah 31:22.

13. Romans 8:20.

14. Romans 8:21.

# Part Four

## The Hidden Power of a Good Wife

*Chapter Eight*

# Abigail: Wise Woman of Intuition

*He who finds a wife finds a good thing, and obtains favor from the Lord.*[1]

In my dream our eyes met briefly as she was led from the city. Strange as it seems, I was in her somehow for that solitary moment. Her deep eyes alert and sad as if she knew she had been born for this day. All those like her, without spot or blemish for three hundred years, had lived out their lives naïve to what might have befallen them. But she had come to the kingdom for such a time as this, and the destiny of all the righteous crowded around me to observe the solemn ritual weighed like the whole world, a millstone about her neck. That neck around which the executioner looped the simple red twine rope by which she was pulled along, down the gauntlet between the rows of onlookers, down into the rough valley, to the place for which she had been born.

I thought I could feel the warm exhalations of the breath of life yet in her as she passed before me, close enough for me to reach out my hand. I could have touched her red hair, a copper and gold blaze rippling under the white heat of noon sun. Eyes wide, nostrils flared, she took in the last smells of the beloved city she would never see again. Did she know it was for that city's jewel, the Temple in the midst of Jerusalem, she would give up her life? For that Temple and for every accused woman, mute, she went. But I cried out within, a wrenching prophetic pain of identification with something ancient, of past and future, when her neck was broken and she went down upon her knees.

The child within me moved, and I awoke. The knowledge of such a temple of great stones in a city not known in Israel was strange to me...but in my dream it was very real.

My name is Abigail, *her father's joy*. I am the wife of a king, pregnant with the king's son. They say the heifer of my dream was sacrificed by Moses after the death of Miriam. The ashes of that cow, still used for the waters of separation, are part of a great mystery. They are used sparingly, so powerful are their powers of purification from death.

In the afterglow of my dream I lay still and silent, pondering the blessing of the Almighty that has come to me. I dwell in peace, a wife of choosing whose name also means "leader of the dance." But it was not always so. I would have taken the ashes of the red heifer into my mouth were my first husband still alive. Let me tell you how I came to this day.

Greed and control are the same. A greedy man must possess all he sees. He will get it by any means and by ownership exercise control over it. Once obtained, however, the object of his desire loses its meaning and he lusts for more. Such is the nature of sin. God forbid men like that come to rule. Control gives a man a feeling of power, and a greedy man will seek to possess more than goods of this world and livestock. I have seen that such men are wont to possess their wives, not out of love but because of greed; that is, the need to have power over them. This kind of greed—the power to possess—can drive him to a certain kind of madness. He becomes like a shrieking bird of prey that falls hungrily upon carcasses in the wilderness. Life flees the soul of such a man, unable to know love, leaving him always empty, with nothing to abate his hunger or his anger.

The cruelest blade of all is the double-edged sword of greed and religion. Such a man was my first husband. A rich man, Nabal did not spare with his offerings to YHWH. He said he competed with heaven to see who could make a greater display, the shepherd of Carmel or the Shepherd of Israel. And he would laugh. Many men in the region had had business dealings with Nabal, and like Jacob with Laban before them, they smarted for any gain they received. In the meantime, my husband became very rich. The ancient proverb says, "From *rasha'* (wicked ones) come *resh'a* (wickedness)." Nabal, *"vile one"* or *"fool,"* is an acronym for the name of another man with his same nature: Laban, *"glowing with wickedness."*

In the first few days after our wedding I saw Nabal glow with wickedness. It lit his face with ire, giving his countenance a darkness like the crack of dry lightning, promising no fruit but destruction. He snatched my hair in his strong hand and bent my neck backward until I was on my knees before him, wondering how I had come there. I thought he was still asleep when Shmuel, his manservant, came to our quarters in Carmel to inquire whether to bring us food. Not desiring to disturb my sleeping husband, I bent close to Shmuel, whispering to bring yogurt and dates and some of the fresh bread I knew was already being prepared for the household. Suddenly, Nabal's enraged face overshadowed me like darkness moving over the land. I thought my neck was about to break under the strength of his grip.

Later, I went to my mother-in-law, and when the veil fell from my face, she sighed and muttered something about my needing to learn how not to stir up the ire that rested like unspent fire in the bosom of her eldest son. And I did learn. But that fire was never spent until the day it consumed him. My failure to give him an heir was another reason my vile husband came to accuse me. He ranted on and on with insinuations about the curse of rottenness in my belly. When he finally prepared to put me to the test before the priests in Nob, I looked forward to it with hope.

Women talk of different things among themselves than do men. Sometimes our talk includes whisperings about the legends of the mysteries of the tabernacle. Few of those mysteries include women. One that does concern women, however, is the ritual involving the ashes of a red heifer. This ritual is known as "the waters of jealousy." I pondered to know how the terrible curse from that ritual took effect and rotted an unfaithful wife's thigh.

You may think it strange that I would contemplate such a fearful thing. But the strange ritual drew me as it was the only possible hope for deliverance from a jealous, vengeful husband whose rage flamed against me like the fires of Gehenna. I longed for those waters to douse the flame of his jealousy, proving me innocent in the face of the priest and making me free from the constant abuse I suffered at Nabal's hand. Even as I nursed the bruises on my face from his "accusations," I waited hopefully for the day when the longed for waters of separation would assuage his jealous religious heart.

During those unhappy months my spirit was encouraged by a recurring dream. It was always the same. I stood before the priest at the waters of separation, drinking the potion he had mixed with the ashes of the red heifer. Immediately after drinking I turned, my soul exonerated and filled with such wonderful peace. Behind me stood Nabal, changed to stone, his stubborn anger frozen forever on his face. I simply walked past him and into the city, free at last, leaving him behind like some stubborn idol of the land still standing in the face of God. But I am getting ahead of myself.

It was shearing time in Israel. The shearers, in great numbers, drove their cutting blades down the thick backs of Nabal's flocks. Like their master, each competed with the other. For all that enriched our house in coin and possessions, our sprawling compound was as empty as my womb had been, all because of my husband's lust to own.

At times I felt the attention of the house servants was as much spying as serving. In his obsession to possess and control, Nabal scrutinized my every action. In the seven unfruitful years since our wedding, I had learned to be a careful steward of my words. I also gained a reputation as one having a bright countenance and keen intuition. All of these traits came at a cost, however, and built an inner strength in me that more than once held me up and sustained me through difficult times.

"My master calls for you, mistress." It was Shmuel. Indentured to Nabal at a young age for debts owed at his own father's death, Shmuel had nearly served out his bond. I did not wish to ponder what it would be like in a few months when he was gone, returned to his home to seek a wife and make a life and family of his own.

The household had been busy since well before sunrise, preparing food for the shearers as well as provisions for the herdsmen in the field. Nabal's holdings were vast. His flocks and herds numbered more than three thousand, and he was the envy of many younger men who lusted for the same power to get wealth that Nabal possessed. Many times I heard them whisper his name when we passed by in the markets where we went to buy Persian spices and trade our wool for spun cloth from Philistia and Egypt.

I took a moment to arrange my hair before the bronze plate Nabal had provided me after our wedding. "To make sure you keep yourself pleasing, as a husband wishes," he had said. Many times during those first few weeks, I wondered if he meant that I was not as he desired since he seldom focused his attention on me unless I neglected my duties or performed them poorly. And when that was the case it was not only Nabal's tongue I felt. "I'm coming now," I said to Shmuel. I followed after his hurried steps to where our master would be waiting impatiently to be served his food.

"The king's men are also in the fields with us," one of Nabal's men was saying as I came and went with my handmaidens bringing their first meal of the day. I didn't listen to all they said, and once they were served and had filled themselves, I withdrew with the other women to the women's tent to eat and to wait in case we were called on again.

The next afternoon I was giving instructions to my maids when Shmuel came hurrying to me.

"Mistress please!" he said. "May I speak with you?"

"Certainly," I said, motioning for him to speak on.

He glanced nervously around the room. "It is a matter of privacy, my lady."

I wiped my hands and gave the bowl of kneading I was nursing over to one of the young serving girls. "Finish preparing this for me," I told her. Shmuel led me outside the house and with a lowered voice reported an ill turn of events.

"The king's men have been residing in the company of the herders," he said. "They have been honorable in all things and their presence has assured the safety of our flocks from Philistine marauders for a season. But now there is news." He looked behind him to make sure no itching ears listened. "Evil tidings!"

In those days there were many rumored tales of the war between the king and soon-to-be-king of Israel. King Shaul's jealousy had turned to bitterness against the Anointed One. While they fought one another, the Philistines kept changing sides, fighting first with one and then the other. David's strength was legend. Yet, had I not learned within my own house that when one who lusts to control cannot, he must destroy instead. King Shaul was such a one.

Shmuel told me that David's men had come to Nabal to ask for simple provisions in return for the wall of protection and peace they had given to our shepherds and flocks. David had requested meat, water and bread enough so that his men did not suffer hunger while they continued to avoid King Shaul and his army.

"What happened?" I asked, although I felt I already knew the answer.

"My lord abused the lads David sent in his name. With a sneer he said, 'Who is David? Who is the son of Jesse? Tell that fox that if his pups want holes in which to lay their heads and butchered lambs to fill their bellies they can beg from some other field besides Nabal's.'"

"And the soon-to-be-king?" I asked, fear rising in me. "What did he do when he heard this reply?"

"Even now he is on his way with a guard of four hundred swordsmen!" Shmuel said, his eyes wide with terror. "By this time tomorrow there will be not one stone of this house left upon the next nor a man left alive!"

"Does my lord know he comes?" I asked.

Shmuel shook his head. "He does not. I am expected to carry this message to him."

"Quickly then," I said. "To the stores. Bring me such as I command loaded upon asses and ready to ride out to meet the king of Israel!" My hands trembled, as did my heart, as I hurriedly gave instructions. "Call me as soon as everything is ready! And tell no one why you are preparing these things. Let them assume it is a feast for celebration ending the shearing time. Wait to report these evil tidings to my husband. Perchance God will show me favor and turn the tide that comes to take us away entirely!"

I took hold of his shoulder. "I owe you a great debt for your faithfulness, Shmuel. I cannot think how I shall ever get by when you leave with the new year."

"You must not think of it," he said. "The day shall have trouble enough of its own. And now we have trouble to attend."

When all the provisions were prepared, I sent them ahead with some of the serving lads to meet David and his men. Shmuel and I followed behind. As we came over the rise, we saw David and his army riding up the wadi, each man with his sword girded at his side and sparing neither sun nor horse. I kicked the sides of my donkey and pressed the animal to bring me down into the midst of the king and his riders. No doubt they were stunned to see a woman and her manservant coming with asses loaded with two skeins of wine, two hundred loaves of bread and five sheep already prepared, plus raisin cakes and figs.

The king told me later that when he saw me, he assumed that these provisions were for the shearers, while he and his men were still being left to go hungry, despite the protection they had provided. The sight caused him to swear an oath: "Surely in vain I kept Nabal's belongings safe from harm in the wilderness and returned nothing unaccounted for! He has returned me evil for good. May God do so and more to the enemies of David, if I leave even one man of his house alive by morning!"[2]

But then he saw my face as I lighted off my mount and ran toward him without fear, falling prostrate in the dust at his feet. "On me myself my lord be all this iniquity!" I cried out. "Accept these provisions for your servants! Pray, allow me to speak a word and hearken to the words of your handmaiden. Let not my lord pay any mind to this worthless Nabal, my husband. For as his name, so is he, a *vile one!* But had I known the soon-to-be-king of Israel had sent to my house I would have made provision sooner!"

Without looking up or pausing I went on, the words I had prepared flowing out of my mouth. Reaching out I touched the toe of his shoe. One of his guardsmen jumped forward and pushed my hand away with his staff. But David put out his hand and stayed the man from removing me further.

"Hold. Let this good wife speak."

"Forgive the rebellion of your handmaiden!" I continued. I kept my eyes on the feet of the king as I spoke to him all that I had prepared in my heart. "When the Lord makes my lord a secure house, and according to all the He has promised, commissioning you as Prince of Israel, may the king be bound up in the bundle of the living and his enemies be flung away in the hollow of a sling!" Assuming the guilt and penalty on myself that moment in the shadow of the valley, I faced death and thought of the red heifer.

The king told me later that in that moment he was dumbstruck. His bent upon the destruction of my house and all those within flowed away from him like a river during flooding season. My words turned the king's mind to his own days as a lad when he had gone out to meet the giant of the Philistines with nothing but five smooth stones and the Name.

Finally, my words spent, there was silence. Even the horses were still. My face was still in the sand. Only the goldcrests chitted and sang playfully to one another as they skittered about in the scrub around us.

Then the king began to laugh. When I looked up and saw his merry face, I too laughed. I couldn't help it. He reached down with his hand and gently pulled me to my feet, brushing away a bit of sand on my lip.

"I am a fool!" David bellowed to his guard. Pointing at me he said, "Blessed intuition, woman! You have prevented me from bloodshed! What is your name?" he asked.

"Abigail, my lord!"

"Your wisdom is a wall about your house, mistress Abigail," the king said. "Go back and tell that dog of a husband of yours that David has spared him because of you. I accept your gifts. But I receive them in your name, not his." When he looked at me I trembled. "I will remember you, wife of a fool, when I come into my kingdom!"

All the way home I practiced the words I would speak to Nabal. But by the time we got there, my husband was drunk from celebrating with the shearers and was beside himself in merriment. I could hear his coarse, raucous voice even before we entered the gate.

"Where is my wife?" he bellowed. His words were slurred from too much wine. "Shmuel!"

I looked sideways at the servant. "Tell him I have gone to bathe. I will perfume myself quickly. Perhaps a good countenance will soften what is to come when he learns of what I have done with his sheep and wine."

Shmuel spurred his donkey into the shed while I went off to prepare to meet the master. In a few more minutes I came into the feast unnoticed by the boisterous company of fifty or so herdsmen and many servants. It was the feast of a king with much rich food and the best wine flowing down the beards as well as the gullets of those who attended. Some of the nobles from the villages were there as well. For now the wine and, no doubt, the certainty of all the profit he would make from his wooling had Nabal in a very good humor. He was leaning to one side, too drunk even to sit up straight. I decided to wait until morning to tell him about David and his men. Eventually, it took two of our biggest, strongest servants to carry him to his bed. That night was like the first I had spent with him, tender and clumsy. And it was the last.

The next morning, as the wine slipped away from him and we lay together just before dawn, his other self asked, "Where were you at the start of the feast?"

My skin suddenly felt cold. All my carefully prepared words fled from me like foxes from a fire in the canebrake. I heard myself say, "I went to David and his men in the wilderness. I have taken them provisions as they requested of you."

I will never forget how Nabal's dark face grew even darker as his rage rumbled like a gathering storm over my words. In the white-hot flame of jealousy he accused me of warming the bed of a rebel while my own marriage bed lay cold and barren, bringing him shame day to day. They were the old accusations only with a new object, not shearers or servants or merchants. This time the king himself was accused.

But the words that once cut and condemned me were no more than rain against stone to me now. Between their strokes he said at last the words I had longed to hear. "In ten days the shearing will be finished. Prepare to answer for your harlotry. I will bring you before the priests in Nob and afterward throw the first stone myself to cleanse Israel of your stain!"

His face, blood-drained from his rage to a sickly white pallor, contorted into a horrible mask of hatred. He shook me hard with both hands, railing on the faulty fabric of my nature. But when he raised a hand to strike me, everything stopped as suddenly as it had begun. The hatred on Nabal's face melted away into a look of utter surprise, as if his breath was suddenly taken away. His arm froze in position, ready to strike, the fingers of his hand locked into a twisted claw like that shrieking bird of prey. Then his face became slack, his eyes rolled back into his eyelids and, wordlessly, he slumped back onto the pallet. A line of spittle dripped down his chin as he clutched his chest and throat.

I called for Shmuel.

Those were ten interminable days. On the morning of the tenth day I rose while it was still dark and went to the mikvah. Scenes of the day of my wedding came back to me as I submerged myself in living waters. Marriage had not been what I had expected, but in recent days the friendship of God seemed to be over me. My heart rested securely. This was to have been the day the millstone of accusation was to be lifted. But the voice of the accuser himself had been cut off. Nabal had not spoken a word since the day he last raised his hand against me. He had been unable to move from his bed since I reported to him the action I had taken with the provisions for David.

Then Shmuel brought me the news. Nabal was dead in his bed, as lifeless as a stone statue. Like the one in my night vision.

Shmuel went to report my widowhood to the king. He intended to ask the king to intercede on my behalf that perhaps a faithful man of Caleb's tribe would cast the shoe for me in mercy. With no family of my own and no brother of my late husband to fulfill his obligation, I would be destitute. I didn't care. I was free from a cage of dread and despair. I entrusted myself to my God knowing He had opened the cage Himself and from it I would fly.

Shmuel confided to me that when he heard the king's reply, he laughed out loud in spite of himself.

"Send to Nabal's widow, servant," David had said. "Tell her the king will arrange for a marriage to secure her future."

"To whom sire?" Shmuel had asked. "There is no brother of my lord Nabal."

"The king himself," David replied. "A wife of her countenance will get me favor from on high!"

The child in my belly moves again. I smile. I shall call him Chileab; *"protected by the father."* God is my Judge.

## Endnotes

1. Proverbs 18:22.
2. 1 Samuel 25:21.

# Chapter Nine

# *Binah*: The Power of a Woman's Intuition

Nabal didn't know how good he had it!

He had wealth, power, influence—but his character was too poisoned by greed and lust to enjoy them. Morally and spiritually, he was a "low-life" who could not fully appreciate his privileged position. Truly, Nabal was as foolish and worthless as his name suggested.

This is borne out by the fact that he completely failed to recognize and appreciate the most precious treasure in his house: his wife, Abigail, a woman of great compassion, intellect and insight. Abigail was an assertive, brave, and highly intelligent woman who was not afraid to take responsibility, no matter the consequences. Most importantly, Abigail had an unbreakable faith in God. She trusted Him with her life and her welfare. She looked to Him for strength and guidance to live under Nabal's evil authority and even, if necessary, she trusted Him to bring about a change in her circumstances.

In truth, Nabal's behavior toward David and his men was inexcusable. Ingratitude for their help and protection was bad enough, but to answer their request for food and drink with rejection and contempt violated all accepted codes and customs of hospitable conduct. Hospitality is one of the most important and time-honored customs in the Middle East. Failure to extend hospitality when asked would cause a family to lose face and subject them to the scorn of the community. The custom of hospitality was so ingrained that even if an enemy came to your house and requested shelter, you were honor-bound to receive him and protect him as long as he was under your roof—even to the cost of your own life.

This is why Lot refused to release his two house guests to the men of Sodom, even offering to turn over his two virgin daughters instead.[1] And it is why running out of wine at the wedding feast in Cana created such a crisis. By turning water into wine, Jesus protected the bride's family from a great social embarrassment.[2]

So Nabal's behavior was more than just rude; it was an impudent insult. Nabal certainly knew the custom of hospitality and what was expected of him. He simply refused to play along. In the face of such a snub, no wonder David was ready to spill the blood of every male in Nabal's household!

Fortunately, Abigail had a more graceful spirit than her husband. As soon as she learned of Nabal's rebuff and that David and his men were on their way to wreak vengeance, she grasped immediately the nature of the problem and knew right away what needed to be done. Where did Abigail gain such insight? Why was she so much more astute on such matters than her husband? The answer lay not in her knowledge of the custom of hospitality or in the power of her intellect, which was formidable, but in her very makeup as a woman. As we would say today, Abigail's insight was "written into her DNA."

Women are intuitive by nature and, generally speaking, endowed with it to a greater degree than men. The phrase "woman's intuition" is proverbial even in our sophisticated modern and postmodern society today. But it is more than just a proverb. Intuition is one of the distinctive qualities that sets women apart from men and is the source for much of the unique perspective and contribution that women can bring to any setting. In fact, this intuitive quality is a natural part of a woman's "voice"—the voice given her by God. In the Old Testament, the Hebrew word *binah* is used to refer to this uniquely feminine intuition that was meant to function much like the Holy Spirit. Eve's shortfall was that she followed her desires, rather than the innate wisdom, *binah*, which the Lord had given to her. She didn't steward her vessel in keeping with the nature of the Giver. The vessel is to be fitted to and serve the anointing and power placed within it, not the other way around. But, the fulfillment of Joel after the cleansing of Calvary restores women, including this characteristic of God's intuition specifically fashioned in women.

## *Binah*: Right-Brain Spirituality

In the beginning God spoke all things into being from that which was not made; that is, out of nothing. This speaking—the Voice of the Lord—went forth as a "breath" (*ruach*) or Spirit that infused life into all living things, especially our first parents in the Garden of Eden. This is the Voice that Moses and the Israelites heard thundering from Mt. Sinai and that Elijah heard as a gentle whisper at the mouth of the cave.[3] It is the Voice that John and others at the Jordan River heard when Jesus was baptized.[4] The Voice is the essence of God Himself activated to effect His will in the moment. At Pentecost, God put this Voice in the church—male, female, young, old, bond, free—without distinction or restriction. Pentecost is the redemptive restoration of the Voice of God to His people.

God's Voice is literal light and sound waves of the Spirit—and here we enter the shadow realm of quantum physics. Quantum physics, or quantum mechanics, which has revolutionized our understanding of how the universe functions, deals with the behavior of subatomic particles. These sometimes appear to behave like particles and at other times like waves, depending on how they are being observed or tested. Unlike classical mechanics, which seeks precise values for every object and any given instance, quantum mechanics takes a more probabilistic view. In a way, we could say that quantum mechanics is the *intuitive* side of science...the right-brain counterpart to the left-brain focus on precision and exactness...a balance for truth in the inexplicable realms where faith presides.

Similarly, *binah* is a concept in Judaism concerning an innate wisdom formed in Eve as she was made from the matter taken out of Adam. *Binah* is the "right-brain" side of God. Eve subjected the *binah* within her to the desire of her eyes at the tree in the garden. In other words, she *ignored* it. She went against her better judgment and was deceived. Her sin resulted in her subjection to her desire and ultimately, her being ruled by her husband. Thus began the precedent and pattern of female subjection and male domination that has characterized most of history. In the process, Eve (and women in general) lost much of the capacity for influence and authority their intuition (*binah*) could have afforded them. With a few very notable exceptions that capacity was not restored until Pentecost.

Just as God divided man and woman physically, He gave each one separate roles to play, which combine to produce spiritual completion for the couple. Man's sphere was the external world, while the woman's sphere was as the instiller and protector of the vital inner self and internal values of her family, particularly her children. She was entrusted with developing, shaping and building the ethical, moral and spiritual personality of those in her charge. The mother is the "caretaker" of the soul, determining the spiritual destiny of each child and safeguarding the spiritual balance of the future generation. These responsibilities are, of course, shared by the father, but because of their essentially intuitive nature, they are especially suited for the woman, endowed as she is with the quality of *binah*.

In traditional Jewish understanding, *binah* is associated with a woman's influence and authority such as to cause others to "listen to her voice." It is connected to wisdom of a kind that enables women to "see" the truth or reality of something that is not as clearly or as quickly obvious to men, who generally are more factually or logically oriented. Stated another way, *binah* is the ability to discern critical differences between situations or entities that on the surface seem similar. The word *binah* comes from the Hebrew root bin, which means "between." *Binah*, then, refers to a woman's innate ability to "read between the lines," so to speak. It also defines some of the unique aspects of the mind of God and His heart formed in women.

Essentially, *binah* has to do with the power of discernment. An ancient Jewish blessing reads, "You [God] have given the rooster *binah*, [i.e. the ability] to distinguish between night and day." In other words, a rooster can discern the arrival of day even while it is still dark—and announces his discovery to the world! The rooster knows a situation not for how it looks, but for what it truly is. This ability exemplifies *binah*. It also explains why the condition of a woman's soul is essential to the stewardship of a woman's power.

This is part of woman's uniqueness that caused Adam to exclaim, "She is it!" when he first laid eyes on Eve. The woman was designed to complete the man and, as this side had been taken out of him, the presiding involvement of the woman balances the table of insight, wisdom, thought, and power in any matter the man undertakes. She was originally to be at his side to work and to watch over the garden of creation. She lost that position at the fall. Christ, the "second Adam," has restored woman to her rightful place at man's side as counterpart and helper.

The fulfillment of Joel's prophecy at Pentecost restores woman to her rightful place and role, including this characteristic of God's intuition that has been specifically put in the woman.

Release of the woman's "intuitive voice" has great significance for the revelatory, intuitive and authoritative realm of spiritual things. This restoration, however, is possible only through the infilling and Lordship of the Holy Spirit.

As women traverse the journey back to Eden and God's original intent, it is the voice of the Holy Spirit that will resonate with the intuitive nature God built into each of his female creations. He is the witness that speaks truth and identity into each of us. This is not only true as we seek to reverse the abuses and oppression of women by the religious and social barriers put in place by the traditions of man, but it is especially true for women, who like Abigail, find themselves in a situation of severe physical and emotional abuse. Such is the testimony of Celia.

Co-dependent, dysfunctional, abuse, and neglect are all terms descriptive of the home environment Celia was raised in. By the time she was seven, Celia was the principle caregiver of her younger brother. She used a stool to reach the sink to do the dishes and the laundry. Her parents were physically violent and emotionally volatile; there were seasons without assurance of whether there would be money for groceries or rent. At 16 Celia sought escape from the pain of her homelife. She married her 19-year-old boyfriend. Within two years her stormy marriage ended in divorce. That began a lifestyle spiraling into alcohol and drug use, in and out of relationships, until she found herself literally under the boot of a man determined to kill her out of sheer rage.

"I was twenty years old, living in the small town where I grew up, running with the worst people, hurting, angry, proud and completely lost. Looking back I realize that I just wanted to be loved and cared for, but I was with a man who was just as violent and volatile as the family I grew up in. At first the abuse was emotional. He began to play on my insecurities by suggesting that "I might be pretty enough, skinny enough...etc. to be loved." He began stripping away every vestige of my identity with his constant criticism and suggestions that I might be able to please him if I would do this or change that, always something different from what I was or what I did. Then, the violence began. The first time he beat me, it was, ironically enough, because he thought I was too pretty. After months of tearing me down, now his jealousy raged. By this time I was in a vicious cycle. I had lost what little identity and confidence that I had had, and if I made any hint that I might leave, he beat me. The one time I did leave, he forced his way into my home and for five hours of terror he beat me mercilessly.

In the midst of this, I was also pregnant with his child. Every person in my extensive family had urged me to abort the baby. Despite the lifestyle of drugs and abuse that I was living and my own family's dysfunction, they were too proud to have their name shamed by my pregnancy and illegitimate child. Only one person, an aunt, urged me, no insisted, that I not abort the baby. But when she said I should give the baby up for adoption because I was not in any condition to be a good mother, something inside of me rose up. "She wasn't going to tell me what to do with my baby!" I made an appointment to end my pregnancy. All the time I continued my lifestyle of wild parties and heavy drug use, because I wasn't planning to have the baby. I had been to the clinic once and was told to come back for more counseling before the procedure. Then, on the day that I was scheduled to have the abortion, they needed to do an ultrasound because I had waited so long. For some reason, when the practitioner was doing the ultrasound, I asked to see. She, of course, said no. But before she could stop me, I grabbed the machine and whipped the screen around. What I saw shocked me—there was my child! It was a living baby! The nurse quickly turned off the machine and hustled me to the abortion room. I was so shaken from the tiny life I saw that I didn't know what to do. On the table I trembled as the doctor came to take my baby. I tried to say something, "Umm... I'm...not sure...I."

The doctor stepped back from where she was examining me, lifted her mask and said in a bitter growl, "Then get off my table!" With nothing on but the examination gown, I ran out of that room. I found my things and threw on my clothes. Shaken and crying, I ran from the building.

It is the grace of God that I did not abort my child, but it caused me to be completely rejected by my family. I soon found myself utterly alone in our small town, working and trying to survive often on canned beans with no one to care whether I was afraid or in need. But the turning point came just a few months after the birth of my child. It was the most frightening night of my life. Up until this point, even though my boyfriend was very violent and had almost superhuman strength, he abused me in such a way that most people would not see the evidence. On this night, however, his fury unleashed with no holds barred. I had gone to meet him at a party. Because I looked "too good" his jealousy began to rage. When he wanted to go to another party, I said I was going to go home. Further enraged that I was going to leave, he forced me into his car. He began abusing me as he drove furiously around town. We pulled up to various gatherings where his friends were loitering outside. I already had a black eye and it was obvious that he was in a violent rage, but despite my appeals and screams to call the police no one came to my aid. At last he sped out of town toward the mountains. He grabbed my hair at the back of my neck and began to slam my face against the floorboard of the car. All the while, he was speeding recklessly up into the mountains. In between head slams, I could see the speedometer. We were going upward of 90 miles per hour on a winding mountain road. I didn't know which was going to kill me first—his hand or his driving as we careened off the edge of the mountain. He was completely out of control physically and emotionally. He began to tell me that he was going to murder me. Already having endured several hours of hell and abuse in the car, and on my way to certain death, I prayed: "Lord, if you will get me out of this I promise I will leave this man." It was so intense that I couldn't even move—I was just hanging on to survive. Then I suddenly didn't care anymore. He had pushed me to such an extreme that I went beyond fear. I was already dead as far as I was concerned. Turning, I got in his face. "Go ahead!" I screamed. "Do it now! Kill me!"

Something broke at that moment. He reached over. I was sure he would kill me. Instead he started to hug me. I was numb. My instinct was to survive—whatever it took. Without emotion I let him hug me. Then he turned the car around and drove back to where my car was parked. Stunned and numb from that night of hell, I walked to my car. I remember the sun had just begun to rise on the horizon as I drove home.

It took another month for me to leave him. I was desperate and was searching for anyone to help me and my baby. I was looking for anywhere and anything I could do. I was determined that no matter what happened or who rejected us, that we would survive together and I would be a good mother. Through a miraculous series of events I was able to enroll in university and find my child and myself a place to live. I had escaped the abuse and was making strides toward a better life. But I had not yet escaped from my history—I was still driven by the voices of my accusers tormenting me and abusing me. For two years, I was flat—out miserable. I was drowning in depression, often suicidal, and suffering multiple addictions. This all intensified to the point that I began to be afraid I was going insane. I remember thinking, "I need someone to pray with me." Somehow from my limited knowledge of God, I knew that I needed to run to Him and let Him hold me and comfort me. I wanted to hear His voice.

I decided to call the aunt that had urged me not to abort my baby. I asked to visit her. During that visit I was baptized in the Holy Spirit. The Lord met me in such a powerful way my mind couldn't understand it. A language that I didn't know came gushing out of my mouth. At the same time, He began to heal my heart. I was instantly transformed, set free and delivered.

I can say with confidence that God heals and redeems us from even the worst the world, the devil and the flesh can offer! He has healed my heart completely. The pain of my experiences has been turned into victory in my life. I have faith and a testimony of the power of God for others who are struggling. He has not only restored my life, but that of my family as well. I love my parents, my child, my church and my generation! I am living a stable, productive, exciting, faith-filled life, raising my child and building the kingdom of God. From the moment I was filled with the Holy Spirit, one of my highest joys has been prayer. Now I am part of a church where my child and I are a part of consistent, committed, corporate prayer in the context of my church family. To any woman who has struggled with abuse and anger, be encouraged; there is hope in the Lord. The only way to victory is through Jesus. Open up your broken gates and let the King of Glory come in. He will come and fill you with power to transform and restore every place in your life. I have found a key to my restoration has been the power of the in-filling of the Holy Spirit. He is the Spirit of Truth and Liberty. After a lifetime of abuse, the Holy Spirit delivered me from bondage and replaced the voices of the accuser with Truth. Believe in God; He is the God of miracles of which I am a living testimony. No matter what you are struggling with, lift up your eyes and look at the Lord. On a practical level, be connected to a body of believers that can come along—side you and encourage you as you walk out of the old patterns of abuse. And be thankful in every situation. Thankfulness looses miracles—and I am a walking one!

Where the Spirit of the Lord is, there is liberty. Dead religion and church traditions have covered the vision of women like the veil described in 2 Corinthians 3:14. But the Holy Spirit has come to minister life, identity and transformation into the hearts and minds of women. It is time for the veil to be taken away, revealing the identity of the glorious Bride, male and female together, set free from the condemnation, strife and identity crisis that began when Adam and Eve found themselves naked in the garden.

## Shaping the People of God

Throughout the Old Testament we find numerous examples of godly women who used their *binah* intuitive nature to help shape the people of God and move history in the direction God intended. Sarah is one example. At first she encouraged her husband Abraham to father a child and heir by her handmaiden Hagar because she herself was barren. After her own son Isaac was born, however, Sarah later insisted that Hagar and Ishmael be sent away to protect Isaac's place as heir. This was more than simply a mother's preference for her own flesh and blood. Even when Abraham was reluctant to send Ishmael away, Sarah intuitively knew that the future of her family—and God's people—lay with Isaac, not Ishmael.

Rebekah, Isaac's wife, showed the same intuitive discernment with regard to her sons Esau and Jacob. Although Isaac understandably favored Esau, the firstborn, Rebekah discerned that Jacob was the one through whom the nation God was building would come. She had heard the Voice of the Lord while her sons were still in the womb, telling her God's divine order. This helps explain, at least in part, her scheme with Jacob to deceive Isaac into giving the all-important blessing of the firstborn to him instead of Esau. She had heard the Voice of the Lord while her sons were still in the womb, telling her God's order.

Jacob, in turn, marries Leah and Rachel, daughters of his uncle Laban. After many difficult years working for his uncle and enduring Laban's dishonest treatment while he himself remains honest throughout his employment, Jacob prepares to return to his home in Canaan, prompted by the command of God. Before leaving, Jacob asks Leah and Rachel whether they should leave on good terms with Laban or depart abruptly. Both of his wives advise Jacob to sever all connections with their father immediately. They, like Rahab, Jael and Ruth after them, discern the destiny and promise on the seed of Abraham and choose to leave the land and ties to their family for the blessing of Israel. Jacob heeds their counsel and they all depart abruptly, in the middle of the night.

We have already seen the intuitive astuteness of Rahab, Deborah and Abigail and the roles each played in God's redemptive plan for the ages. Anna, who we meet briefly in the Gospel of Luke, is a New Testament woman who displayed great *binah* in her discernment of the true nature of the infant Jesus.

Each of these women possessed the ability to see what was not obvious on the surface; in this case, distinguishing and recognizing the spiritual validity of something. That is the essence of *binah*. And this innate feature built into the woman by her Maker is an ideal wineskin in which to carry the power and Voice of the Lord.

## Donkey Vision

Sometimes God uses the simplest and humblest objects to teach us the greatest lessons. For example, much of our understanding of binah and how it works in our lives is illustrated in the story of a humble donkey—Balaam's donkey.

You remember Balaam. He was a non-Israelite prophet whom Balak, king of Moab, hired to speak a curse against Israel so that he would have victory over them. Four times Balaam tried, and four times he was allowed to speak only the message that God gave him—a message of hope and blessing and promise for Israel.[5]

Although Balaam spoke the Word of the Lord on these occasions, he was basically a pagan who worshipped all the local gods of the land. And he was no particular friend of Israel. Balaam was more like a "hired gun"; he sold his prophetic services to the highest bidder. When he was unable to curse Israel as Balak desired, Balaam found another way to be useful to the Moabite king. Numbers 31:16 reveals that Balaam's counsel helped the Moabites draw the Israelites into idolatry, bringing God's judgment upon them.

Balaam's efforts to fulfill Balak's commission to curse Israel give rise to one of the most peculiar and remarkable stories in the Bible—the story of the donkey that talked. Balak attempts to hire Balaam, but God appears to him and tells him not to go or to curse Israel because they are blessed. Balaam obeys and declines the commission. Balak tries again. This time, God tells Balaam he can go but must speak only the words that God gives him. Here is where the story takes its peculiar turn.

*So Balaam rose in the morning, saddled his donkey, and went with the princes of Moab. Then God's anger was aroused because he went, and the Angel of the Lord took His stand in the way as an adversary against him. And he was riding on his donkey, and his two servants were with him. Now the donkey saw the Angel of the Lord standing in the way with His drawn sword in His hand, and the donkey turned aside out of the way and went into the field. So*

*Balaam struck the donkey to turn her back onto the road. Then the Angel of the Lord stood in a narrow path between the vineyards, with a wall on this side and a wall on that side. And when the donkey saw the Angel of the Lord, she pushed herself against the wall and crushed Balaam's foot against the wall; so he struck her again. Then the Angel of the Lord went further, and stood in a narrow place where there was no way to turn either to the right hand or to the left. And when the donkey saw the Angel of the Lord, she lay down under Balaam; so Balaam's anger was aroused, and he struck the donkey with his staff. Then the Lord opened the mouth of the donkey, and she said to Balaam, "What have I done to you, that you have struck me these three times?" And Balaam said to the donkey, "Because you have abused me. I wish there were a sword in my hand, for now I would kill you!" So the donkey said to Balaam, "Am I not your donkey on which you have ridden, ever since I became yours, to this day? Was I ever disposed to do this to you?" And he said, "No." Then the Lord opened Balaam's eyes, and he saw the Angel of the Lord standing in the way with His drawn sword in His hand; and he bowed his head and fell flat on his face. And the Angel of the Lord said to him, "Why have you struck your donkey these three times? Behold, I have come out to stand against you, because your way is perverse before Me. The donkey saw Me and turned aside from Me these three times. If she had not turned aside from Me, surely I would also have killed you by now, and let her live." And Balaam said to the Angel of the Lord, "I have sinned, for I did not know You stood in the way against me. Now therefore, if it displeases You, I will turn back." Then the Angel of the Lord said to Balaam, "Go with the men, but only the word that I speak to you, that you shall speak." So Balaam went with the princes of Balak.*[6]

How's this for irony: Balaam the "seer" could not even see the peril he was in from the Angel of the Lord! His humble beast of burden saw the Angel, however—as well as the danger—and tried three times to take her master out of harm's way. All she got for her trouble were beatings and abuse. It was not until the Lord "opened the mouth of the donkey" and she spoke to Balaam concerning his mistreatment of her that Balaam finally saw what the donkey saw—and fell to his face in fear.

This *female* donkey displayed *binah*, the ability to see and comprehend something in the spiritual realm that her male master, despite all of his supposed prophetic prowess, could not see. Her insight saved Balaam's life three times.

## Donkey Wisdom

Balaam's donkey has become one of our personal heroes. She encourages us with the humble, often subtle, yet power-filled way God weaves women into His awesome acts. During a low point in Bonnie's inner life as a woman, God used the story of Balaam's donkey to lift her up and give her a new perspective on life:

At the time, I was distracted by what was going on inside of me. Like Martha, I was encumbered with much serving. I was anxious and bitter and did not understand what was happening in the eternal realm. I was too focused on what was happening to me in the temporal realm.

It was a number of years ago, when all of our children were still quite young. Mahesh was away sometimes 250 days out of the year ministering, and it was my job to hold down the fort, literally, raise the kids and take care of the ministry and all of those sorts of things.

One evening Mahesh was home and our family was sitting together and reading the One Year Bible. The particular reading for that day happened to be the story of Balaam's donkey. Mahesh was a firm believer in making God and Bible reading fun for our kids, so he assigned all of them different parts of the story to act out. Serah was the Angel of the Lord's presence, Anna was the narrator, our oldest son, Ben, the big guy, was the donkey and our youngest son, Aaron, the little guy, was Balaam.

Mahesh and the kids were busy reading and acting out the story and having a great time while I was basically asleep on the couch. The kids were playing this story to the hilt. When the time came for Balaam to beat the donkey, Aaron, remembering all the times his big brother frustrated him, really let Ben have it. I won't even tell you what Serah was doing as the Angel of the Lord's presence, with a chance to lord it over her brothers!

All I wanted was for the story to end so I could put the kids to bed, finish the laundry, and go to bed myself. About the time they were finishing the story, I heard what could have been an audible voice saying, "Bonnie, you're the donkey." The voice had that strange quality about it that made me feel that it was about to really change my life, to revolutionize something, to dump me out of my box of anxiety, bitterness and self-pity.

The voice spoke to me so clearly that I knew immediately I had to pay attention to this story. A little later I went back and read it—and saw myself in that donkey's life. The first thing I noticed is that the donkey was a "she." That struck me in such a way that I began to see Balaam's donkey as a spiritual type for women. Donkeys are beasts of burden. Donkeys carried judges, prophets, and priests. Jesus rode a donkey when He entered Jerusalem. A donkey carried Jesus with His parents down into Egypt to save them from Herod's murderous rampage. The donkey is God's humble messenger and servant.

When I heard the Lord say, "Bonnie, you're the donkey," I said, "You're darn right, I've been the donkey—and that's exactly how I feel tonight!" Then He opened my eyes and helped me see some things differently. That very night the Lord delivered me from a spirit of slavery. Something changed in me that took me from the place of being Martha, who said, "Jesus, if You had been here he wouldn't have died," to being Mary, who said, "Jesus, Your presence gives me life."

He began to work in me the understanding of the ministry of reconciliation. He began to teach me the meaning of being conformed to the image of Christ[7] in the fellowship of His suffering and the power of His resurrection.[8] He began to show me the importance of trusting Him and keeping my mouth shut until such a time as His presence stood in the way and I was compelled to speak.

Balaam's donkey never had a voice until that day and moment when it was needed. The prophet was so intent on his revelation and his mission and fulfilling his commission that he was not sensitive to the true nature of the spiritual environment. But the donkey was simple, innocent and fresh and so saw the Angel of the Lord's presence. In a similar way I believe that in the coming months and years women will be a key to understanding the times we are living in, so it behooves us to be concerned about Him and about discerning what He is doing around us. We need to be connected.

## Intuitive Wisdom for Critical Times

Balaam's donkey is a picture of a servant, the burden bearer, with no title, no authority and no will of its own. What a donkey does have is strength, endurance and a broad back. The prophet Balaam in this story can represent a lot of people or a lot of things in your life: the ungodly people for whom you work, the pastor or elders you serve even when they walk in the flesh, perhaps even your spouse. Like the donkey, you are called to serve faithfully and without complaint. If you focus on being sensitive to the Lord and His presence, He will make a way for you and the day will come, as with Balaam's donkey, when He will give you a voice. Humility, self-control and faithfulness are attributes of the King and are the qualities of His burden bearers to whom

He gives His voice. Your personal history is preparing your for your kairos moments in God's destiny.

Consider the lesson of Balaam's donkey: she was not focused on the temporary. She wasn't even preoccupied with the weight of the man riding on her back. She saw only one thing: the Angel of the Lord's presence. Even the prophet himself did not see that at first. It is possible that the Holy Spirit might speak to you before He speaks to your spouse or to others in your family. It is possible that you may sense the pressure of a needed change in your life before the authorities in your life see it. It is possible that you may be in the fear of God and know Him and be moving according to His presence, and He will press you, and you will move against the wall looking at Him and may inadvertently "crush the prophet's foot" along the way. In other words, when you follow the Lord, you may rub some folks the wrong way. They may not understand at first what you are doing or where you are coming from. Some of them will never understand.

Don't let that stop you. Be like Balaam's donkey. She wasn't worried about anything except responding to the Lord's presence. There is great wisdom here. We have shared Bonnie's "donkey story" many, many times in conferences and other places, and have never yet met a woman who did not relate to it, or receive some understanding from the Lord that helped her on her way in wisdom and in power.

Scripture uses a donkey, a servant and beast of burden, to represent the tribe of Issachar. As we saw in chapter seven, the anointing upon the sons of Issachar was twofold: they discerned the times and they knew what Israel ought to do in those times. The blessing spoken of Issachar was of a twofold prophetic anointing that would give them authority in God's pasture, the sheepfold, as His shepherds, because they discerned the "pleasant land" of His inheritance.

In our day, the "sons of Issachar" are those who understand the Kingdom of God and lay down their lives for its advancement.

The donkey that carried the prophet Balaam was given a voice. The donkey that carried Jesus into Jerusalem in triumph, revealing Him as Messiah, facilitated the cleansing of the temple. Those burden bearers carried the anointing. The oil that soaks the wicks and lights the lamps with fire is the Holy Spirit, the Light that shines in the darkness and speaks better things than Sinai and the fulfillment of Pentecost.

The flames of fire that sat upon each one at Pentecost and caused them to utter the prophetic words of the Lord are falling from heaven in this hour. They rest upon the daughters and maidservants of the Lord, the keepers of the flame of Pentecost. The Lord is restoring woman's voice! As His spokespersons, our voice is just as powerful as the Voice revealed in Psalm 29:

> *The voice of the Lord is powerful; the voice of the Lord is full of majesty. The voice of the Lord breaks the cedars...The voice of the Lord divides the flames of fire. The voice of the Lord shakes the wilderness.*[9]

A new day has dawned. It is time for Deborah to join with Barak and for them to enter upon the battlefield. It is time for Balaam's donkey to have a voice. It is a time for a woman to encompass a champion. To all God's children, and especially to His daughters, let us say this: *you are priests and kings. No spiritual office or spiritual gift is closed to you.*

Centuries ago, in the midst of a culture where the priesthood was limited to men of a particular family lineage, the prophet Joel said:

> *And it shall come to pass afterward that I will pour out My Spirit on all flesh; your sons and your daughters shall prophesy, your old men shall dream dreams, your young men shall see visions. And also on My menservants and on My maidservants I will pour out My Spirit in those days.*[10]

Pentecost *is* the redemptive restoration of the VOICE of God to men *and* women. The Voice is the essence of God Himself activated to effect His will in the moment. Restored by the power of Christ and His resurrection and filled with the power of the Holy Spirit, women are coming into their own with the full force and influence of their God—given *binah*, partners in accomplishing the will of God on earth *as it is in heaven.*

## Endnotes

1. Genesis 19:4-8.
2. John 2:1-11.
3. 1 Kings 19:12.
4. Matthew 3:16-17.
5. For the full story of Balaam, see Numbers chapters 22-24. For the record of his death at the hands of the Israelites, see Numbers 31:8.
6. Numbers 22:21-35.
7. Romans 8:29
8. Philippians 3:10.
9. Psalm 29:4-8.
10. Joel 2:28-29.

# Part Five

## The Hidden Power of a Praying Woman

*Chapter Ten*

# Anna: Prophetic Woman of Prayer

*Now there was one, Anna, a prophetess, the daughter of Phanuel, of the tribe of Asher. She was of a great age, and had lived with a husband seven years from her virginity; and this woman was a widow of about eighty—four years, who did not depart from the temple, but served God with fastings and prayers night and day. And coming in that instant she gave thanks to the Lord, and spoke of Him to all those who looked for redemption in Jerusalem.[1]*

There are people in our lives who are really *Hashem* in disguise, or at least it is He who has put them there to be His voice, His hands, His wisdom to mold, change and direct us as He would do. My Yoreh was one such person. A righteous one. We called her that because she was like the early rain that precedes winter, both blessing the earth and seed for planting and warning the people to paint their roofs and make ready for harsh weather to come. She was my mother's sister and had been widowed while very young. They called her a prophetess. My Yoreh had lived many years under the vows of a Nazarite, a holy one devoted constantly to God. She spent many days in the Temple in Jerusalem, devoting herself there to prayers and fasting in the company of others who came and went keeping the vows.

Our tradition says, "He who has not seen the Temple of Herod has never known beauty." Every devout person in Israel turned to its stream of living water for nurture and refreshing. The hosts of Israel celebrated their great religious feasts within its courts. Sacrifices, forgiveness of sin and sanctified souls were all bound together in the bundle of the living. The faithful assembled beneath its porticos to learn the law of salvation and to renew their vows to the Most High. The altars bled with the blood of the sacrifices offered by the priests, the fragrance ascending to heaven on clouds of smoky incense. In its center, behind the tapestry veil, once a year the high priest made atonement for the sins of the people. On occasion fire had descended from heaven to consume the offering. The Temple was a city within a city.

Once, the Divine Presence, the *Shekinah*, had dwelt visibly between the cherubim that hovered with golden wings over the coffer. But never in my lifetime had it been seen to fill the Holy of Holies or overshadow those expansive courts. In fact, it was rumored the ark itself had been removed to some other place in days before my time. Angels did minister before that house's altars though. They were seen by some and occasionally there were miracles. Visions and the spirit of prophecy rested upon some who worshiped and served within.

Aunt Anna was one of these. She loved the temple and she loved the holy city, but she loved YHWH more than these and lived a holy life devoted to Him, separated from all sin. The thing I remember most about her was her serenity and joy. Her gnarled hands, though soft, would curl around my small ones as she took me with her to the Court of Women for her daily prayers. Even when she was old, which she was even when I first knew her, my Aunt Anna was young and it seemed she would live forever. Now I know, in spite of what the Sadducees argue, that she will. I still hear her voice and the influence and strength of the things she taught me are the foundation I stand on every day.

I have such vivid memories of accompanying Yoreh to the place she loved, the Temple. Sukkot was the most joyous times of them all. One year, Eemah stayed behind because she was still in her time of purification after the birth of Rachael. Only Jochanan, the eldest son of our family and I, the eldest daughter, came with Yoreh and Abba to celebrate the drawing down of the water. My siblings, three of them then, were very young and difficult to keep all together in such a melee. They stayed behind with mother and a servant so they wouldn't get lost in the festival crowd.

The courts were filled with every kind of holy sight and sound. Incense and sweat, smoke from the Nazarites cooking fires together with the blood of the sacrifices, whispered prayers, songs, laughter and repentance of the humble all mingling together as one community. Within the enclosed rectangular space scores of worshipers at a time assembled easily and conveniently. They entered from all sides of the city through one of its many gates, according to their origin and intention for coming to Jerusalem's crown.

Herod's Temple contained many courts and devoted areas. In addition to the public areas were holding areas for the oxen, sheep and doves that were sold for sacrificial purposes. Living quarters housed the servants of the Temple. The Court of the Gentiles around its outer perimeter was like a huge market place. Jews and Gentiles alike sold their wares along with items to be used for offerings. Food vendors and merchandisers came and went, spreading out their tables or setting up their booths. You could buy anything in the world at the Temple in Jerusalem.

People came to Jerusalem and the Temple from everywhere. There were black-skinned, brown-skinned, and olive, as well as soldiers, fair skinned with fair eyes. And there were always the scores of beggars sitting in the garments assigned them by the priests, confirming their disabilities and granting them the right to beg for alms.

Bodies pressed together and milled about in excited jubilation on that great and final day of the Feast. We gathered for the water libation. The pinnacle of joy. It was also the first year Jochanan went with Abba into the Court of Israel instead of with Yoreh and me to the women's balcony. I can still see his self-satisfied side-wise glance at me as he straightened his shoulders and followed Father off through the crowds. I never could quite understand why his going closer to *Hashem* drew him away from me. Up until that moment Jochanan and I were best of friends even though brother and sister. But after that he changed and spoke to me in a condescending manner, always dismissing me as if I was now second class to his new status among the men.

Yoreh didn't seem to take much notice of his airs. She drew me along towards the stair that led to the balcony erected on three sides above the Court of Women. It had been built during Yoreh's lifetime. "'Too much levity,' they said," Yoreh told me as she described the time when the sages first forbade women to mix with the men during the water drawing celebration. The Great Rectification they called it. "No matter," Yoreh said. "The Lord God will come suddenly to his Temple and set His house in order."

We passed beneath the great lights, four candelabras whose bowls were higher than the Temple walls. Several young *cohen-im* struggled hurriedly to pass great buckets of oil up the ladder positioned against one of the lampstand posts. They poured the golden stuff into the bowls under the disapproving gaze of an old priest berating them in harsh whispers for the fact the lamp should have been filled by now. The young carriers were not much older then my brother and some were less in height and strength. Yoreh smiled at them and looked at me, the light of her eyes shining happily. "Asher shall dip his foot in oil!" she laughed, drawing a connection between the blessing of our clan and the oil the *cohenim* in training were bringing out from the chamber of oil to fill the lampstand. "A city set on a hill, Rivka! Every doorway in Jerusalem will be lit from this court. The court of Women!" And Yoreh would smile as if she knew a secret whose time had not yet come. As if once the One we waited for appeared even the fate of our gender would unfold in glory. Indeed, our own threshold glowed with the faint warm glint of the great lamps whose wicks gave their light over the temple walls during Sukkot.

We made our way up the moving channel of human bodies passing up the final stair just as the trumpet sounded below. With a great joyous percussion of instruments the Levites led the parade of worshipers down to Siloam to draw the water for the altar. "Therefore with joy," the Levites began to sing aloud, "shall you draw water from the well of salvation!" I stood on tiptoes and leaned forward between eager women and their children who like me were trying to see the fire jugglers as the music and the dancing began. Trying to be polite but anxious to see what was going on often meant an elbow in the ribs or a disapproving clicking of the tongue from someone's mother if I was too for-ward in my eagerness. We pressed ourselves into the bank of women and children trying to get a good view of the festivities below.

"Do you see Jochanan, Yoreh?" I asked.

"No, child," she answered. "But be sure he is there with the men. He is officially one of them now!"

The past winter my brother had been mitzvah'd. Now a son of the covenant, he was received into the community as an adult. My own mitzvah was coming in the next year but I knew it wouldn't make a difference in allowing me to go with Abba to worship because, as Jochanan always reminded me after that, I was *just a girl and the Court of the Israelites was the place only for men!*

Then, I remember the day that I first met *Him*. The thing I recall most clearly about that day was not He but my Yoreh's face as His mother allowed her to take the babe ever so briefly into her arms. It was as though the air around us changed, electrified with the Presence that used to go with the ancients into the Holy Place. I remember it also because it was at the time of the early rain. I loved that time because Aunt Anna had taught me to look for it as the sign of answered prayers.

Her heart was rejoicing as she went with me up the causeway steps past Siloam's Pool. A sweet soft mist softened the air and darkened the cold limestone beneath our feet causing it to give up its slightly earthy smell. They had been building the Temple complex for half of Anna's life. She loved to describe how each new section of the glorious house appeared under the hands of the master craftsmen. She loved this dwelling place of God and had devoted herself to it with her whole life.

Just as much, Yoreh loved this city. David's City. "Israel's crown," she would say, smiling with a look as though her soul was embracing the whole of it and gathering it within her arms like a hen her chicks. "My beloved Jerusalem is the center of the universe." Then she would recite the psalmist, sometimes singing the words. *"If I forget you, O Jerusalem, let my right hand forget its skill! If I do not remember you, let my tongue cling to the roof of my mouth—if I do not exalt Jerusalem above my chief joy."*[2] Then, turning to me, she would remind me, "The Anointed One for whom we wait will enter here, child. Be certain of that. For *Hashem* will fulfill His promise to save His people from their sins. In that day all those who oppress us will be shut outside the gates of this city!"

Standing in the court looking out the Eastern Gate after we had dropped our half-shekel into the trumpets of the treasury, she would point. "There, He will come to His temple through those very arches." Every time I passed the view of them, my heart would thrill, expecting any day we would see Him. And at last, on that one day, we did. But not as Zechariah promised, "humble and riding on a donkey." At least, not on that day. He looked rather like my little brother Adam at the time, a tiny squirming human, sucking his fist and staring at all the strangers looking at him. Still in swaddle and just as old as the end of his mother's purification, with his father looking as old as my aunt, I saw Him.

It was in the month of *Chesvan*, and *Hashem* had answered the prayers for rain offered during the great feast the previous month. Yoreh and I had just dropped our shekels into the treasury trumpet when we heard old Simeon's voice coming from the chamber where lepers and women came to be purified. Yoreh and I turned to see Simeon take the babe in his arms, a look of heaven's light on his face. "Sovereign Lord, as you have promised," Simeon cried, as tears flowed out of the wrinkled corners of his eyes, "now dismiss your servant in peace! For I have seen your salvation which you have prepared in the sight of all people." He held the child up and I wondered that the infant did not cry out though his arms and legs straightened for a moment like all babies when they are suddenly thrust on high! "A light for revelation to the Gentiles and for glory to your people Israel." The child's father and mother looked at each other with the strangest look, as if these were not the first such things said of their son. Yoreh had that same look on her face. Then she did something she had never done before. She dropped my hand and I had to run to keep up with her.

Simeon then blessed the babe's parents. Turning to the woman, he spoke more softly, as with compassion. "This child is destined to cause the falling and rising of many in Israel, and to be a sign that will be spoken against. The thoughts of many hearts will be revealed." I couldn't hear what he said at the end.

Something about a sword. And as he said that, Yoreh began to prophesy.

I never saw Him after that. I grew up and Anna grew ancient. We almost changed roles in those last years, for it was I who led her by the hand up the causeway to her daily prayers.

And then she was gone.

The first morning I came to the Temple alone was poignant. I suppose I had not realized how large her presence had been to me. In the evening we had been with her by her bed. Anna put her gnarled, old soft hand over mine. "The Consolation of Israel has come, child! I now go in peace to meet you on the other side! Remember what I have taught you and be faithful! I am not afraid of death, for even it at last shall be put under His feet." With her last breath she told me, "Pray for the peace of Jerusalem. They will prosper who love her." Then Yoreh smiled and fell asleep.

I ran to my father and buried my face in his arms. He scowled at me when I looked up through my tears, vowing to live as she had lived, separate and consecrated to *Hashem*. "From this day I will give myself to *Hashem*, to His city and His temple as she did!" I cried.

Abba touched my hair and said, "Yoreh was widowed by the will of *Hashem*, child." Then he quoted to me the blessing of our clan as Yoreh used to do. *"Let Asher be blessed with children; let him be acceptable to his brethren, and let him dip his foot in oil."*[3] YHWH, blessed is He, has a good husband and many children for you."

The next year I was welcomed as an adult into the community. Then I saw Rueven for the first time. Actually, I had seen Rueven almost every day of my life until then, for we had always been playmates and had grown closer as Jochanan became so pious. But that day I saw him! I was so happy when it was determined that Rueven and I were to be engaged. As Abba told me, my path was different from Yoreh's but I follow in her footsteps of faith. I give my devotion to *Hashem* and His city, a temple within my heart day to day when I cannot go to this one made of stone and gold. Yoreh's influence and her prayers are always with me, her pathway of learned wisdom and the fear of the Lord sustaining me.

I now have a family to care for that keeps me from coming here as often as she did. I hold the knowledge in my heart that I am watching over a generation and molding Israel's future even as Yoreh did me. And so I have peace and joy in my duties toward my husband and my children. We have three daughters, fine and sweet. And now Hashem has given us a son. It is the Feast of Dedication. I have just finished my own days of purification and we have come as His parents did that day when I was a child, to dedicate our first son to YHWH. We paid the money for two turtledoves into the treasury trumpet as our Judah's purchase price, then made our way up the fifteen steps to stand before the great Nicanor Gates as the priest announced his blessing on our child.

Standing on the threshold of the doors before the middle wall of partition, I feel a thrill in my heart that at last *Hashem* had given me a son. One day, one of my own children will be allowed to enter into the inner courts as Jochanan had. As I stand there I can see out through the gate over the Kidron Valley and the arched roadway where they used to lead the red heifer. For a moment, I am sure I feel Yoreh's presence too, or at least hear her voice: "Unto us a son is given..." She often used those words of David when Anna spoke of the One to come. "To come," she said, "before I see death."

At the moment I think I hear her speaking, there is a commotion behind us. I look up to see only the crowd of worshippers flowing around someone in their midst whom I cannot see because of them. But I know who it is. There is not a soul in Jerusalem who has not heard of Him by now. "The Nazarene!"

some are saying, their voices carrying to where we have finished the blessing of our son.

The babe I saw dedicated here with Yoreh has grown into a man. They say He heals the sick and breaks the yoke of the oppressor, just as Yoreh told me. There are also controversies. Across the terrace a scurrying crowd gathers after Him into the area under Solomon's Colonnade. I hear Yoreh's voice of old:

> *"Nevertheless the dimness shall not be such as was in her vexation, when at the first he lightly afflicted the land of Zebulun and the land of Naphtali, and afterward did more grievously afflict her by the way of the sea, beyond Jordan, in Galilee of the nations. The people that walked in darkness have seen a great light: they that dwell in the land of the shadow of death, upon them hath the light shined. Thou hast multiplied the nation, and not increased the joy: they joy before thee according to the joy in harvest, and as men rejoice when they divide the spoil. For thou hast broken the yoke of his burden, and the staff of his shoulder, the rod of his oppressor, as in the day of Midian."*[4]

Rueven takes my arm, holding our son, our only son thus far, we move into the crowd toward the colonnade to hear Him.

## Endnotes

1. Luke 2:36-38.
2. Psalm 137:5-6.
3. Deuteronomy 33:24.
4. Isaiah 9:1-4.

*Chapter Eleven*

# Daughters of the King

We have all known them. Influencers. Women whose faith, charity, courage, and clarity sowed seeds of eternal destiny in us. Powerful, clear women who were unafraid to worship God and unashamed to speak of Him. Faithful to guide us when we stumble and humble enough to tell us when they do not know the answer. Yet they will be right there next to us, bearing, hoping, believing. They are gifts and they are lifegivers. Women like Anna. True daughters of Eve they are and, even more, they are daughters of the Lion of Judah, the King of the universe.

Such is the destiny of every woman: born to be an influencer for right and good and truth. The full manifestation of the redemption of the woman shall be the last mystery to be fully revealed in Christ as we prepare for His coming.

Created in the image of God in the beginning, and the first in the history of humanity to fall to attack, Eve was also the first to receive God's promise of justification—her Seed. All of this indicates the hidden power of the woman in the plan and purpose of God.

Widowed and with no natural seed of her own, Anna never lost sight of the Seed that would be the Redemption of Jerusalem. She devoted her life to watching, praying and building up the House of God through her influence and service. She set a foundation for the next generation; she recognized the Cornerstone and pointed Him out to all who would hear her.

Like Anna, we know a woman who has not let tragedy at a young age cloud her vision of our Sovereign God. She continues to praise Him and influence others to give Him the Glory due His name. Here is her powerful testimony:

Being a widow at age 27 was the last thing that I thought would happen to me. John died from injuries sustained in an automobile accident. Even in the midst of the trauma and devastation of the accident and seeing my husband struggle for his life, I never imagined that he would die. But, one day before our seventh anniversary, he did.

From the outset of the events that led to his death, I knew the Lord was with us. At the scene of the accident, my four year old son and myself were helped out of the car and watched over by a fireman who immediately appeared on the scene. He called my son by name and told him, "We're going to get you out, boy!" I was able to get out and walk to the road-side where this same fireman told me to lie down. The fire-man stayed to watch over and comfort my son. To this day, my son speaks very highly of firemen. The next thing I remember were the voices of the paramedics around me. When I asked about the fireman later, I was informed that no firemen had responded to the accident! But God had sent this "fireman" to help us and to give my son a sense of security in a time of tragedy.

The trauma my husband suffered was too overwhelm-ing—he went to be with the Lord six days after the accident. We believed he was going to be healed. But for reasons I do not know God had a different plan. In the midst of all of it I just kept trusting the Lord because He is sovereign. After

John died the Lord allowed me to quickly deal with the "why" of his death.

"We don't always have the privilege of asking why," God told me. I listened to this word and made a decision. From that point, even in my worst times, I refused to permit myself to ask God why it had happened. That decision spared me from spiraling into the deep abyss of self-pity and disillusionment. Not allowing my heart to be filled with offense or disbelief made room for the Presence of God. He downloaded into my heart. He tenderly revealed that the only guarantee we have in this temporary life is our eternal salvation. And that the Holy Spirit, the Comforter, will *always* be with us. Jesus didn't say that life would be easy or perfect, but that when we face trials and tribulations, He would be with us.

If I escape to the island of self-pity the Lord brings me back. We don't have the luxury of asking why because we serve such a sovereign plan. If we look through the keyhole of our own experience, however tragic, we won't see God's big plan. Even in his death, I have seen the fruit of John's life touching others. His legacy inspires people to get their lives in order, to restore their marriages, and mend their broken relationships.

The pain of losing my husband is beyond what most people understand. But grief is grief. People can relate to a failed marriage, a lost child, shattered dreams, unfulfilled vision, or broken relationships. My grieving process has been under the skillful hand of the Master Surgeon, carefully, lovingly peeling away layers of pain and trauma, loss and shock. He has seen to it that I not experience it all at one time. He has made it bearable and fruitful. I have felt His comfort and miraculous Presence around me every day. Where I go He goes. At times I have literally felt the hands of the Lord holding me up, physically carrying me forward. Both my son and I miss the joy, the memories and the fun we had as a family together. But the very moment my husband passed into Jesus' arms, I felt God place his arms around me. I loved and served the Lord before I met my husband, and I knew I had to keep loving and serving the Lord after he was gone. The Lord continues to be the strength of my life. I wake up each day and give the Lord thanks for what I do have right now.

The Lord has been so gracious to my son. From the fireman who came to help us till today the Lord has spared him from trauma and fear. We talk about Daddy and the things we used to do. My son has seen me cry, and it has helped him release his own frustration or pain. But the Lord has enabled him to see that we are not alone. We overheard him talking with a friend, another four year old. He said that his dad died and that his dad's in Heaven now with Jesus. The other little boy said, "Now God is your father and God can be your father and mother." My son said, "Yeah, God is my father now." He misses his daddy, but he knows that now he has two "daddies" in Heaven! You can look into his eyes and see the peace. He doesn't have that emptiness you see in many kids traumatized by divorce or other losses in their lives.

There are times when a wave of grief, a release of anger over what has happened or disappointment from unfulfilled dreams that we had of growing old together washes by. There has been a process of reestablishing and refocusing my life as a single mom. I have found complete grace to make those adjustments. Every day by looking to Him rather than looking back, I have a hope. Even in the darkest hours I am aware of sweet assurance for my son, myself, and our future. Knowing John is with Jesus adds comfort. He is a part of Heaven now and he is cheering us on.

God is our Provider. It doesn't take the place of daddy—but makes it easier. After the accident the harsh reality of my circumstance hit home. A single mom and single woman, my own injuries from the accident, creditors calling, the hassles of switching everything into my own name, all came crashing down. At the same time I was betrayed by some friends and I cried out to the Lord. My misery turned to unforgiveness toward those who had hurt me. I said, "Lord I didn't ask for this! You have to help! You have to help me forgive." He said, "I'm your defender." The next day I received an unexpected blessing beyond anything I could have asked for. Shortly after John's death, we were able to give a tithe and offering that had been a goal for us as a family before, but we had not been able to attain before he passed away. As I put the offering in the basket, I looked up to the Lord and said in my heart, "Thank you Lord, we did it."

Because of the severity of my own injuries, for six months my church surrounded me with love and practical assistance: cleaning my house, preparing meals, taking care of my son. I am so thankful for the place that the Lord has planted me in the midst of His body. Thankfulness has been a key to life. I look for things to be thankful for. I refuse to focus on things that are lacking, missing or the way it used to be. Instead I worship and let His glory cover me in the wisdom and grace we need now and for the future!

I know why Scripture says, "He makes the widow's heart sing for joy."

This young woman, like Anna in her devotion to the purposes of God, has refused to let tragedy define her life. Rather, she is focused on building up the next generation and seeing that the legacy of her husband be fulfilled in the life of her son. She has tapped into the hidden power of women essential for the building of the dwelling of the Lord—the power of women to shape and bring forth the living stones of His tabernacle. Like the staves that supported the curtains of the tabernacle, women are essential to the fabric and design of the dwelling of His glory.

## The New Math

One day Mahesh was pondering the communion of the Godhead. Provoked, he asked, "How can three be one?" Then he sensed the Spirit of God ask him, "How are you doing the math?" Mahesh replied, "1 + 1 + 1 = ...3." Then he sensed the Spirit say, "With just a slight change, you will understand." Mahesh said, "What do you mean?" The Lord impressed Mahesh to change the equation to "1x1x1 = 1." Suddenly, Mahesh realized that mathematically, three can be one. All Three in perfect communion multiplies power exponentially, yet the result of the equation is still One. Like the Godhead, we were designed for communion and unity, expressing the fullness of the image of the Three-in-One God we were created to reflect. It is a mystery with a clear face. God created women as an integral part of the equation for mankind to rule with power and dominion over creation. Women, redeemed, released and fully involved in the affairs of God and man produces exponential results. We live in a multi-dimensional world, and without the hidden power of women, mankind is missing a key to the equation to fulfill the purpose and dominion He created us for. At Pentecost, the power of the Holy Spirit was restored to every man and woman who would believe, accelerating the purposes of God on the earth. In like manner the exponential power of women multiplied into the equation will bring forth the fulfillment of God's original design and will for mankind. Then we will see "one chase a thousand, and two put ten thousand to flight."[1] It is time for exponential advancement of the Kingdom through the recognition and inclusion of women and her power hidden through the ages.

A wonderful way to present the entire woman in salvation's story is in a picture that truly is worth more than a thousand words. The mystery of the red heifer sacrifice. It is a mystery because the Jewish sages who stewarded this essential ritual confessed that its revelation was hidden from them. Even Solomon said he could not know it. But we find that at the appropriate time God unfolds His secrets. One of those secrets is His intention for woman.

## The Red Heifer and the Temple

The mystery of the red heifer sacrifice has confounded the sages of Judaism since it was instituted to sanctify the tabernacle under Moses. The keepers of the promises of God's inheritance who stewarded this essential ritual confessed that it is hidden from them. Even Solomon said he could not know it. But at the appropriate time God reveal hidden mysteries. Because this sacrifice was made in the body of a female we have chosen its importance to further reveal the hidden power of the woman. According to the biblical mandate, the ashes of a red heifer are necessary in order to carry out the religious rituals in a rebuilt Temple. The rebuilding of the Temple, the reinstatement of the priesthood and reinstitution of the sacrifices all depend upon the ashes of the heifer. If there are no red heifer ashes, there can be no *waters of separation* and thus no sanctification. The waters of separation were so called because when they were sprinkled upon a vessel, man, woman, or inanimate object, the subject was no longer separated from God or His holy community. The waters of separation from the ashes of the red heifer made the blood of the sacrifices effective in ratifying the reunion they provided.

The essentiality of reunion cannot be understated. Reunion is the only state by which the glory can return. The glory is holy and thus it cannot dwell in an unclean house. The glory radiates out of communion between God and man and thus it does not dwell in a divided house. In Judaism the red heifer sacrifice is essential to this reunion. It indicates woman is essential and included with reunion of man to God. In God's covenant the

female is essential in all matters of His ritual, the house, its spiritual offices and services. Until the time of reunion and the
sprinkling of the waters of separation, technically Israel is cut off
from God and His glory is in exile.

The red heifer sacrifice is a prophetic type of Christ's provision for sin and judgment. In it we see full symbolism of the
restoration of the essential presence of woman, the female in the
Garden, to the place she was built for beside man in service and
dominion over the works of God. Once she is reunited, the whole
community of God, His house and His glory, will be raised up in
glory. This essentiality of the inclusion of woman in the ritual
sacrifice is put forth in God's command even before the law of
Moses. God told Abram, "You descendants shall be as the stars…
and as the sand." To make provision and solidify His covenant
God said "bring Me a heifer three years old."[2] Three years signified the fulfillment of the ministry of Christ, our High Priest, cul-
minated in the offering of His body in death on our behalf. He,
who in a mystery, was slain before the foundation of the world,
before the sacrifices of earth that symbolize Him, was depicted
by God in the body of a female in the first covenant sacrifice.
Why? The female was the wife representing man as the wife of
God. She was the life-giver. Without her there would be no heir.
She was the glory. In communion with her man became complete. With her, the three, man, woman and God became one.
The fellowship and dominion they enjoyed at first was restored.

> *And when birds of prey came down upon the carcasses,
> Abram drove them away. As the sun was going down, a deep
> sleep fell on Abram; and lo, a dread and great darkness fell
> upon him. Then the LORD said to Abram, "Know of a surety
> that your descendants will be sojourners in a land that is not
> theirs, and will be slaves there, and they will be oppressed for
> four hundred years; but I will bring judgment on the nation
> which they serve, and afterward they shall come out with
> great possessions.*[3]

The promise would not be fulfilled without a fight! Darkness and hell would be stirred up to resist the manifestation of the sons of God as His heirs. In the symbols of God's covenant with Abram even before Isaac and the ram, God foretold the history of the human race and His salvation though faith. God would ultimately provide His own Son to deliver Abraham's seed from the bondage and oppression. God would break the yoke and it would never again come upon the neck of His beloved.

Bloodguilt was dealt with in the body of a heifer:

> *And the elders of the city which is nearest to the slain man shall take a heifer which has never been worked and which has not pulled in the yoke. And the elders of that city shall bring the heifer down to a valley with running water, which is neither plowed nor sown, and shall break the heifer's neck there in the valley. And the priests the sons of Levi shall come forward, for the LORD your God has chosen them to minister to him and to bless in the name of the LORD, and by their word every dispute and every assault shall be settled. And all the elders of that city nearest to the slain man shall wash their hands over the heifer whose neck was broken in the valley; and they shall testify, "Our hands did not shed this blood, neither did our eyes see it shed. Forgive, O LORD, thy people Israel, whom thou hast redeemed, and set not the guilt of innocent blood in the midst of thy people Israel; but let the guilt of blood be forgiven them." So you shall purge the guilt of innocent blood from your midst, when you do what is right in the sight of the LORD.*[4]

After the death of the first woman priest, Miriam, the sister of Aaron, the red heifer sacrifice was introduced by God and instituted in the sacrificial cult of Moses under the law:

> *Now the LORD said to Moses and to Aaron, this is the statute of the law which the LORD has commanded: Tell the*

*people of Israel to bring you a red heifer without defect, in which there is no blemish, and upon which a yoke has never come. And you shall give her to Eleazar the priest, and she shall be taken outside the camp and slaughtered before him; and Eleazar the priest shall take some of her blood with his finger, and sprinkle some of her blood toward the front of the tent of meeting seven times. And the heifer shall be burned in his sight; her skin, her flesh, and her blood, with her dung, shall be burned; and the priest shall take cedarwood and hyssop and scarlet stuff, and cast them into the midst of the burning of the heifer. And a man who is clean shall gather up the ashes of the heifer, and deposit them outside the camp in a clean place; and they shall be kept for the congregation of the people of Israel for the water for impurity, for the removal of sin. And this shall be to the people of Israel, and to the stranger who sojourns among them, a perpetual statute. Whoever touches a dead person, the body of any man who has died, and does not cleanse himself, defiles the tabernacle of the LORD, and that person shall be cut off from Israel; because the water for impurity was not thrown upon him, he shall be unclean; his uncleanness is still on him. And for the unclean person they shall take some of the ashes of the heifer burnt for purification from sin, and running water shall be out on them in a vessel. A clean person shall take hyssop and dip it in the water and sprinkle it...But the man who does not purify himself, that person shall be cut off from the assembly, because he has defiled the sanctuary of the Lord.[5]*

Isaiah describes the sacrifice of the red heifer prescribed in Numbers 19 when he prophesied, "*He was taken from prison and from judgment, and who will declare His generation? For He was cut off from the land of the living, for the transgression of My people He was stricken.*"[6] This tells of Christ, bound in ropes and led from Gethsemane across the Kidron Valley to be tried and imprisoned before the High Priest Caiphus and then turned over to death.

From the garden where He made intercession and gave Himself up for sacrifice, Jesus could look across the valley through the Eastern Gate into the Temple. Imagine His thoughts as he prepared Himself to suffer the worst punishment, though innocent, to restore to Himself a pure and spotless bride. That night as He gazed down upon the temple Courts through the darkness he would have seen the lights coming through the gateway and looked forward to the day when Bride and Bridegroom would enter into their joy forever. The *shekinah* would come out of exile and fill His temple at last.

The ashes of the red heifer were mixed with water from the Pool of Siloam. (Coincidentally this pool was only rediscovered in Jerusalem in 2005—another sign that we are coming full circle in our redemption in this hour.) Everything from priests to serving vessels had to be sprinkled with the waters of separation made from the heifer's ashes and *mayim chayim*, living water typifying the Holy Spirit, in order for the defilement of death to be removed. The red heifer sacrifice separated the holy from the profane. Only the ashes of this complete sacrifice mixed with living water could purify those separated from God by sin and welcome them, sanctified, back into the community. The elements of the female as life giver and the living water as a type of the Holy Spirit are representative of God's resolution of what took place in Eden. This redemption would be made effective by the Holy Spirit. Joel's spoke of this resolution when he foretold the eventual outpouring of the Spirit upon all flesh. The sacrifice represented Christ's body, His temple, prepared and holy, made up of male and female reunited in one in Him and receiving Him back in holy fellowship as Adam and Eve once had in the beginning. After the first woman and man ate from the tree that had been forbidden them in Eden sin and judgment entered when God came looking for them in the breezy time of day. God said to Eve, "*In will greatly multiply your sorrow and your conception; in pain shall you bring forth children; your desire shall be for your husband and he shall rule over you."[7]* The heifer declared the seed of a woman would crush the serpent's head and restore God's glory to creation.

Throughout the history of God's people, a total of nine red heifers have been sacrificed, all prior to Christ. In Christian theology it is well accepted that the red heifer sacrifice typifies Christ. Jesus was the tenth "red heifer." He was sacrificed for the sanctification of His Temple. His suffering and death purchased her reunification with God. Jerusalem is waiting for the fulfillment of all this ritual accomplished: a holy house, cleaned and in order where God and His glory will return to dwell forever. John saw the New Jerusalem, a bride prepared for her husband coming down from God. In the meantime the church in the earth has become His temple and His wife to be. The number ten signifies perfection of divine order. By command of God, the only acceptable animal for the red heifer sacrifice was a female virgin without spot or blemish which had never borne a yoke. Since divine order is the core concern in the debate of women's roles and is the principle debate in Christian women's issues, it is relevant for us to examine the red heifer mystery, in which the perfection of the divine order in Christ is depicted in a female sacrifice.

The pure red, native-born heifer would be led through the Eastern Gate over an arched bridge that spanned the Kidron Valley to the *Place of Burning* located just below the northern summit of the Mount of Olives. From that place on a direct line from the entrance to the Temple through the Eastern Gate, the heifer would be bound and thrust into a pile of firewood prepared for the ritual. This was the vision Ezekiel saw by the Chebar River while an exile himself in what is now modern day Iraq—the place of the ancient Garden and the place of the new war. From there he saw the glory of God returning to from exile. "Then He brought me back to the outer gate of the sanctuary which faces toward the east, but it was shut. And the Lord said to me, 'This gate shall be shut; it shall not be opened, and no man shall enter by it, because the Lord God of Israel has entered by it; therefore it shall be shut."[8] Jerusalem sat in need of redemption like a woman with an issue of blood, separated, unable to commune with her husband, waiting for the day of her cleansing. God tells Ezekiel, "I will not hide My face anymore; for I shall have poured out My Spirit on the house of Israel,' says the Lord."[9] Ezekiel saw a man with a scarlet cord and a measuring rod in his hand. Beginning and ending at the Eastern gate Ezekiel watches as the man thoroughly measures everything within the complex, each chamber, every door, window and all its furniture.

> Afterward he brought me to the gate, the gate that faces toward the East. And behold the glory of the God of Israel came from the way of the east. His voice was like the sound of many waters and the earth shone with His glory. It was like the appearance of the glory which I saw—like the vision which I saw when I came to destroy the city. The visions were like the vision which I saw by the River Chebar; and I fell on my face. And the glory of the Lord came into the temple by the way of the gate which faces toward the east. The Spirit lifted me up and behold the glory of the Lord filled the temple.[10]

Jesus surely recalled these words of the prophet as He sweated drops of blood in prayers to God there under the olives in the garden in the moonlight. God had prepared in Him a body whose sacrifice would break the curse that had followed the man and the woman all the way from the garden of old. In His voice that night, if one had been able to hear it, the sound of rushing water, a flood of the Spirit about to be loosed because of the blood, breaking upon the place where God chose to put His name.

The priest would slay the cow with his right hand, catching some of her blood in his left. Seven times he dipped his finger in it and sprinkled the blood toward the Most Holy Place which was in full view from the place of burning through the Eastern Gate. As soon as the fire was lit, cedar wood, hyssop, and a scarlet cord were bound together and thrown upon the burning heifer. Later the ashes were divided into three parts. One part was kept in the Women's Court of the Temple as a memorial, another on the Mount of Olives at the place of burning, and a third was distributed to the priesthood for their service in the Temple. The Temple in Jerusalem was Israel's center of unity. Historian and theologian Albert Edershiem says,

> Around this Temple gathered the sacred memories of the past; to it clung the yet brighter hopes of the future. The history of Israel and all their prospects were intertwined with their religion; so that it may be said that without their religion they had no history, and without their history no religion. Thus, history, patriotism, religion, and hope alike pointed to Jerusalem and the Temple as the centre of Israel's unity.[11]

The sevenfold sprinkling signified complete sanctified reunification and union between God and man, the undoing so to speak of the separation created by the sin of the Garden. In Jewish custom separation between clean and unclean was an obsessive religious concern. Uncleanness allowed death to enter the camp. One of the most common symbols reminding Israel of need for separation and cleansing was ni-DAH, the issuance of blood from women during menstruation. Great lengths were developed to separate women because of that issue. Under these rules we empathize with the woman who had been bleeding for 12 years recorded in the Gospels. Everything and everyone she touched was considered unclean. The only way to keep from causing defilement was isolation. Imagine her humiliation and despair. When at last she heard Jesus was healing people she put her reputation and future in the community on the line and went into the crowd to touch Him. Her faith drew such healing virtue out of Him that He felt it in spite of many hands grasping at Him. He turned and said, "Who touched Me?" Then he pronounced her clean. This woman is a type of all women. Separated from birth and unclean under the yokes and restrictions of religion and the sin of our first mother, the church and our society has been hemorrhaging its life blood and has become unfruitful as it has stumbled over the issues concerning women. The hour of our healing has come. God is cleansing His Temple and returning to full communion with her.

The Jewish sages link the red heifer with the sin of the golden calf. Aaron said that the golden calf came out of the fire - causing the Israelites to become separated from God. Moses pulverized the golden calf and threw its ashes into the water. Tradition says that Moses forced the Israelites to drink the water causing a plague of death in the camp. The red heifer was thrust into the fire and her ashes were mixed with water bringing life to the people. Bound and laid with her head facing west, the red heifer was slain and her blood sprinkled. Then her body was burned using dry palm branches to kindle the fire. The cinders of her ashes were beaten with rods and the bones crushed with stone hammers until they were pulverized into a fine dust. Then they would be passed through a sieve and be gathered up to be mixed with living water for use in the cleansing ritual.

The fullness of this sacrifice took on the punishment of judgment for Eve's sin in the garden. Step by step the red heifer prophesied of Christ to come. We can see the redemption of woman fulfilled with each crushing phase. While our salvation lies in blood and body of the lamb slain typified in Passover in Israel, the red heifer reveals the details of that complete sacrifice. It is fitting, in a way, that the details be carried in the body of a female. How like the role of woman whose burden is typically for the details of her home and family day to day. We see in the red heifer the Lifegiver laying down His life for the lifegiver, Eve and her daughters. Who could claim that so great a salvation restricts a woman from full participation in the things of the Spirit as an heir to all that God gives His inheritance. The handwriting of ordinances that were against woman has been fully taken away. The female gender as well as the male was created in the image of God. From Adam's bone the woman came forth. The red heifer indicates that the entire substance of woman, down to the very genetic code of the bone from which she was built, was fully judged and redeemed when Christ gave up His body for her on the Cross. Eve has been reconciled to God. The body of a female, essential to the restoration of the Temple and the priesthood, figures as representing God's wife. How much more has His sacrifice cleansed Adam's wife. The two sayings that fell over her earthly service in the Garden, multiplied conception with pain in childbirth and subjection to her desire placing her under rulership by her husband were rolled up in Christ and dealt with in His trial and suffering of death.

The mystery of the red heifer reveals the essentiality of women in His plan. Like the red heifer, woman throughout history has faced the enmity pitted against her coming from the enemy. In Christ she has gone down into the rough valley because of the tree in the garden. On the tree of Calvary He undid the work of Eden. The neck of her authority broken by old desire and her identity as one made in the image of God was marred and made unrecognizable as He took the accusations, the stripes, the imprisonment, and finally the nails of the cross. Jesus entered the fire of hell to bring her back from judgment. Up from the grave, He holds the key to hell and death. The door He opens for woman no man should shut. The gate to His house is open, and the glory Ezekiel prophesied is coming home to rest.

The Sabbath is observed every week in Jewish households according to the command of God given to Moses. In it the woman lights the lamps and welcomes the glory home. The next 24 hours she is relieved from her labors. Traditionally the rabbis taught that a man should commune with his wife in loving intimacy on

Sabbath evenings. They understood that the *shekinah* which rested between the cherubim that faced one another, their wings outstretched toward each other were all symbols of God communing in holy intimacy with His people. The knowledge of the likeness of the perfect union between husband and wife, instituted by God in Eden, reflected God filling the object of His affection with his Spirit. God has restricted Himself. He has made Himself interdependent upon the human of His creating. It follows that God has made the man interdependent on woman and vice-versa, from heterosexual marriage in the inner sanctum of the home to the center of spiritual service in His church. No man can be a father without a woman. It is the DNA of the Godhead. This is the mystery Paul spoke of. No woman can be a bride and mother without a man. Family, community, church, and society are dependent on the full inclusion of woman. Her voice, her influence, her power and contribution are vital at all levels. The Holy Spirit has filled her to help.

We have been sprinkled with the blood. We have been sanctified with living water. The ashes of His sacrifice have been applied by the Spirit and our days of separation are over. The veil has been rent. Welcome into the tabernacle. God cleaves to His wife and draws her, male and female together, into the embrace and community of the Godhead. This is the mystery. It is fulfillment with produce fruit—a godly heritage and generation that serves Him. The culmination of this mystery is the culmination of redemptive history that began when God stepped into the debacle in the Garden of Eden. John witnessed it in visionary form as he saw the Lamb's wife, the new Jerusalem, come down from heaven and the Lamb enter into her midst as her light so that there was no longer any need for a Temple. The Lamb is the light of the new city as the Temple lit the city of old. The city encompasses the Temple and the Temple encompasses the *shekinah* as a woman encompasses a Champion and fulfills the prophecy of Jeremiah. For the Jews, without a Temple readied for her husband by the sanctifying property of the tenth heifer's ashes, Messiah cannot come to indwell His people. And so we understand the prophetic reality of woman being restored to her place in the perfection of divine order. It took place in the sacrifice of Christ on Calvary. It was ratified in His resurrection on the third day. Any prohibitions against women then are traditions of man, not works of God. The lost voice of woman, in all her power and glory, is being restored!

The power of death has been broken. The leaven that entered the soul of mankind was purged in the spotless body of Christ who exchanged Himself for woman as well as man. We see it as He becomes the red heifer. A female body laid down, her neck broken and her body burned, a complete sacrifice. Both of these, the neck that holds the head, and the body being given up, are types of woman's history since Eden. The ashes of death the red heifer provided, mixed with living water, and the blood of life the Lamb of Calvary spilled were for cleansing and reconciliation. The end result is resumption of full communion with God and man. Like the middle wall of partition, Christ has taken away all that separated us from our Father and one another.

## "But I am no man!"

As we return to the truth of God's creation of women in the Garden, let us draw another illustration from the Tolkien classic, *Lord of the Rings*. Another daughter of royal birth and great destiny, Eowyn, the daughter of a great king is a warrior at heart. Eowyn depicts the woman who hears the voice of the Lord urging her toward her calling for the sake of her family, her community, her God and her generation. As the 'menfolk' are called out to battle against the dark tide trying to destroy the land Eowyn longs to go and fight along side them. Because she is a woman she is left behind. But that does not stop her. She dons a knight's armor and joins the troop disguised as one of the king's men. On the battlefield the king is felled and the dark Nazgul lord appears to have the upper hand. Eowyn rides forth to confront the dark power:

"Then out of the blackness in his mind he thought that he heard Dernhelm speaking: yet now the voice seemed strange, recalling some other voice he had known. "Be gone foul dimmerlaik, lord of carrion! Leave the dead in peace!"

A cold voice answered: "'Come not between the Nazgul and his prey! Or he will not slay thee in thy turn. He will bear thee away to the houses of lamentation, beyond all darkness, where thy flesh shall be devoured, and thy shriveled mind be left naked to the Lidless Eye.' A sword rang as it was drawn. 'Do what you will; but I will hinder it, if I may.'"

The evil lord draws his power from an ancient curse that protects him from every man who would oppose him. The curse says 'no man' can overcome him. As Eowyn steps out in the appearance of a man the dark lord mocks her, trusting in the curse:

"'Hinder me? Thou fool. No living man may hinder me!' Then Merry heard of all the sounds in that hour the strangest. It seemed that Dernhelm laughed, and the clear voice was like the ring of steel. 'But no living man am I! You look upon a woman.' The helm of her secrecy fallen from her, and her bright hair released from its bonds, gleamed pale upon her shoulders...A sword was in her hand, and she raised her shield against the horror of her enemy's eyes...A swift stroke she dealt, skilled and deadly, the outstretched neck she clove asunder, and the hewn head fell like a stone. Backward she sprang as the huge shape crashed to ruin, vast wings outspread, crumpled on the earth; and with its fall the shadow passed away. A light fell about her, and her hair shone in the sunrise. A cry went up into the shuddering air, and faded to a shrill wailing, passing with the wind, a voice bodiless and thin that died, and was swallowed up, and was never heard again in that age of this world."[12]

There is power in the voice of a woman. And there are some things in this world and in the plan of God that only women can do. In the restoration that even now the Spirit of God is beginning to bring about, women who have been denied or shut off from their rightful heritage and destiny for years are starting to come into their own. They are claiming their inheritance. They are taking their place.

## The Power of the Voice

The Bible says *"out of the heart the mouth speaks."* As God heals the heart issues of His women they are finding their voice. As they find their voice they will also find power: power to rout the enemy and protect the inheritance of future generations. Power to bring a uniquely feminine but godly insight and wisdom into the church and into the social, cultural, and moral affairs of humanity. Power to speak in a way that will influence her eternal destiny and that of her children.

The history of the Holy Spirit from Pentecost forward until the tradition of man crept back upon God's work after the first century and a half after Pentecost shows the choosing and appointment of women as church leaders without contradiction or reservation. Future generations, however, adopted a stance of anti-semitism in an attempt to sever Christianity from the "evil" influence of the Jews, who were viewed as contenders against Christ. Many of those church fathers held explicitly anti-woman dogmas and delivered them into the church theology and tradition.

As the Holy Spirit is not the author of confusion, He has come at last in our day to keep His promises and set the record straight concerning woman made in His image! We have come to the "new thing" Jeremiah prophesied in fulfillment of God's promise to Eve: a woman shall encompass a champion. A renowned Christian leader replied to the questions of a woman minister on the theological issues of women as leaders: "Perhaps we need some Baraks who will humble themselves, especially when God raises up the Deborahs of this world to do what some men cannot do as well."

The prophet Zephaniah spoke by the Holy Spirit concerning salvation using the terms of a woman being visited by her God:

> *Sing, O daughter of Zion! Shout, O Israel! Be glad and rejoice with all your heart, O daughter of Jerusalem! The Lord has taken away your judgments, He has cast out your enemy. The King of Israel, the Lord, is in your midst; You shall see disaster no more. In that day it shall be said to Jerusalem: "Do not fear; Zion, let not your hands be weak. The Lord your God in your midst, The Mighty One, will save; He will rejoice over you with gladness, He will quiet you with His love, He will rejoice over you with singing." "I will gather those who sorrow over the appointed assembly, Who are among you, To whom its reproach is a burden. Behold, at that time I will deal with all who afflict you; I will save the lame, And gather those who were driven out; I will appoint them for praise and fame In every land where they were put to shame. At that time I will bring you back, Even at the time I gather you; For I will give you fame and praise Among all the peoples of the earth, When I return your captives before your eyes," Says the Lord.* [13]

We see the hidden power of the woman a central figure in the beginning of humanity, at its fall and, if God does anything according to His usual way, we shall see her again a central figure in His redemption plan as it comes full circle. In the Tolkien tale we used earlier to illustrate the Spirit-led woman, Princess Arwen deals with her heart issues and makes some difficult choices in order to be a contributing part to the great destiny unfolding in her generation. As we move toward the end of the age and the great marriage of the Son of God the hidden power of the woman is being revealed. The fulfillment of age old prophecy is accompanied by signs in the heavens confirming and attesting to what God is doing. Power is being restored to his church and He is not leaving his women out! Princess Arwen's advent begins in a battle in a watchtower where, like the biblical sons of Issachar those who knew the times and seasons and what should be done had gathered. When Frodo was wounded in the battle, Arwyn saved the day by riding him to rescue and safety. Her mother's instinct and kingly heritage together with the power in her voice put her in a strategic position in her generation. It was the end of a dark era and the beginning of hope.

In America an unusual phenomenon occurred in Death Valley in 2005. It was a sign of the Lord's visitation for all who had eyes and ears to see and hear. Unusual rains soaked the otherwise barren soil and touched seeds that had not been seen for a hundred years. The desert bloomed in glorious color. That same season brought the centennial of Azusa, the great outpouring of the Spirit in Los Angeles that spread Pentecost around the world. On Mother's Day as we completed *The Hidden Power of a Woman*, the *Watchman* comet streaked through space delivering 'babies' in multitudes of stars and scattered them into the night sky. The heavens are declaring the works of God. The earth is singing, "Prepare the way for His coming. Make His pathway straight. Let every low valley be exalted and every high hill be brought low before His face." God is lifting His daughters up out of the dust. He is bringing down the proud strongholds that have been raised against them. God is pouring out His Spirit upon His handmaidens and calling them to take their place. We hear women's voices singing in the rain. They are bringing their strength, their faith, their courage, and their gifts to the battle. The great lights are raised, filled with holy oil; they are shining out from the women's court of God's dwelling place once again. Let every home and heart be illuminated with His Presence. Let the desert bloom and the dry wastes become His garden. Those who know their God will do exploits and His daughters will rejoice in glory.

## Coming Full Circle

The unfolding of the ancient prophecies of the likes of Joel and Jeremiah are coming together with the testimony of God through women in the Old Testament, Jesus' life and ministry, and the advent of the Spirit of Life at Pentecost, to do the new thing promised of the Father. We have come full circle in the greatest story ever told. The human bride is being readied for the appearance of the heavenly Bridegroom. Jesus began His ministry at the behest of a woman at a wedding. He will culminate His work in the wedding to beat all weddings: His own.

As we draw ever nearer that day, He has saved the best for last: the full restoration of the woman as intended in the beginning when God made her in His image! The events of Eden stripped woman of the honor given her by God. The results have been catastrophic. In hanging stripped, abused, abandoned, the weight of sin fully upon him, Christ, dishonored in her stead, has won back woman's honor. The steward of His Kingdom, the Holy Spirit, is returning the honor she was initially crowned with in the unfolding of the hidden power of the woman God made in the beginning.

This wholeness transcends human limitation and societal mores stemming from the traditions of man, be they religious or not. It surpasses human desire as metamorphosis occurs, beginning with the new birth and continuing through the sometimes painful struggle of being conformed to Christ's image again by obedience and mortification of those desires and all else that are not consistent with His perfection. As the hidden power of God emerges in the woman who fully follows Christ, get ready for empowerment in the church, redemption in society, miracles in the body, and blessings on the human race unequal to any previous generation.

A professor of history and religious studies at Penn State, wrote in the *Atlantic Monthly* that Christianity is the religion currently undergoing the most basic rethinking and the largest increase in adherents. He states:

> For obvious reasons news reports today are filled with material about the influence of a resurgent and sometimes angry Islam. But in its variety and vitality, in its global reach, in its association with the world's fastest-growing societies, in its shifting centers of gravity, in the way its values and practices vary from place to place...it is Christianity that will leave the deepest mark on the 21st century.[14]

And Christian women will be among the mark makers! Women in particular have a great deal to learn from and benefit from in terms of the history begun by God and the hidden power of the first woman. Likewise, it behooves both men and women in our day to take a look at some of the things we have believed by traditions that are more the distillation of accepted mores of former times than they are of God's ordination.

Intention, design, promise and destiny formed of God in the beginning are unfolding less like the first rays of morn and more like the noon sun that slips now quickly to brilliant fire before the setting. A Bridegroom is coming for a Bride and they will live happily ever after. In the meantime, the child-bride has grown up to discover she is a woman, the hero has deposed the evil dragon, and the sleeping kingdom is rousing itself to awaken with the dawn. Then at last they shall see one another face to face. The eyes of those lovers will meet: the Second Adam, the wounds inflicted to give up a side of Him to form a Bride still fresh, and the one for whom He slept, clothed in glory, rushing to meet Him.

Until then, like Abraham's servant sent to find her, the Rushing Spirit of God who crowned them in the beginning with glory and honor, has come. His camels with him are loaded with treasure for the woman he has found. Out of the baggage the servant draws gifts to adorn and reveal her hidden power.

It's the breezy time of the day again. God, clothed in the power of His rushing Spirit, has gone out for His constitutional in the Garden of His creation. In the folds of His coat he carries *kol isha*, the woman's voice, the voice He gave her in the ancient garden of pleasure. Getting her voice back has been an arduous journey fraught with many tears. But as He did in days gone by, the Champion has set His face toward His city. She shall be rebuilt.

A man, a woman and their God comprised the first family. They are the foundation stone and building block of all human community, secular or religious. The events of that family's lives have affected every family under Heaven since. While it may be argued there is nothing new under the sun, it is also true that there is a time for everything.

So it is with the unveiling of the hidden power of the woman. Her power, influence, and insight stolen in Eden and hidden for subsequent ages were heard again two thousand years ago when Christ cried out, "It is finished!" and laid His life down. The new thing God began when He made a woman as the crowning glory of His creation work, like the new thing He did as He poured out the Promise of the Father in Jerusalem 50 days after Jesus rose from the grave, is now unfolding. Where we are today has a great deal to do with where we began in human history. Where we are heading is guided by knowledge of our past. We know where we are going. Isaac's wife, bedecked and on camel back, is almost home. From the field where He walks at eventide, the Son looks out and sees her form, a corporal mystery of male and female fully enjoined and empowered in His image as they were at the beginning, light against the dark horizon. He sees her coming toward Him and whispers, His voice carrying to her on the wind, "Rise up my love, my fair one and come away!"

## Endnotes

1. Deuteronomy 32:30.

2. Genesis 15:5, 9.

3. Genesis 15:9-15.

4. Deuteronomy 21:3 Revised Standard Version.

5. Numbers 19:1-20 RSV.

6. Isaiah 53:8.

7. Genesis 3:16.

8. Ezekiel 44:1-2.

9. Ezekiel 39:29.

10. Ezekiel 43:1-5.

11. Alfred Edersheim, *The Life and Times of Jesus the Messiah*, (Peabody, MA: Hendrickson Publishers, 1993), 3.

12. J.R.R. Tolkien, *Lord of the Rings*, ch. vi., p. 874-75.

13. Zephaniah 3:14—20.

14. Philip Jenkins, *The Atlantic Monthly* October 2002; The Next Christianity; Volume 290, No. 3.

Additional titles in the *Hidden Power*
series by Mahesh and Bonnie Chavda:

*The Hidden Power of Healing Prayer*
*The Hidden Power of the Blood of Jesus*
*The Hidden Power of Prayer and Fasting*
*The Hidden Power of Speaking in Tongues*

Available at your local Christian bookstore
or online at www.destinyimage.com

Additional copies of this book and other
book titles from DESTINY IMAGE are
available at your local bookstore.

Call toll free: 1-800-722-6774.

Send a request for a catalog to:

## Destiny Image₀ Publishers, Inc.
P.O. Box 310
Shippensburg, PA 17257-0310

*"Speaking to the Purposes of God for this
Generation and for the Generations to Come."*

## For a complete list of our titles,
visit us at www.destinyimage.com